Christianity and Entrepreneurship

PROTESTANT AND CATHOLIC THOUGHTS

Samuel Gregg and Gordon Preece

THE CENTRE FOR
INDEPENDENT
STUDIES

1999

CHRISTIANITY AND ENTREPRENEURSHIP

PROTESTANT AND CATHOLIC THOUGHTS

Samuel Gregg and Gordon Preece

CIS Policy Monograph 44

THE CENTRE FOR
INDEPENDENT
STUDIES

Published September 1999 by

The Centre for Independent Studies Limited.
PO Box 92, St Leonards, NSW 1590
E-mail: cis@cis.org.au
Website: www.cis.org.au

Views expressed in the publications of The Centre for Independent Studies
are those of the authors and do not necessarily reflect the views of the
Centre's Staff, Advisers, Directors or Officers.

National Library of Australia

Cataloguing-in-Publication Data:

    Gregg, Samuel J. (Samuel John), 1969-
    Christianity and Entrepreneurship: Protestant and Catholic thoughts

    Includes index.
    ISBN 1 86432 045 1

    1. Entrepeneurship - Religious aspects - Christianity. 2.
    Christianity and economics. I. Preece, Gordon, 1954- . II.
    Centre for Independent Studies (Australia). III. Title.
    (Series : CIS policy monographs ; 44).

    261.85

Contents

Foreword

T he figure of the entrepreneur receives a decidedly mixed press throughout much of the Western world, not least from many religious writers. As noted by the authors of this book, there is a distinct tendency on the part of some religious thinkers to regard business practitioners as effectively guilty of questionable practices until proven innocent, or as engaged in an activity which, while materially useful, has little real merit in itself. For most of this century, for example, the Christian churches have given much thought to the role of paid employees and trade unions, and lavished much praise upon them. Until relatively recently, however, Christian thinkers have said much less about entrepreneurship and businesspeople, and much of their commentary has been decidedly negative.

This imbalance in both focus and praise is somewhat questionable. Given that entrepreneurial activity is at the heart of wealth-creation, without which all of us would be quickly reduced to poverty, business activity is surely as worthy of sustained and serious theological reflection as any other form of economic activity. In an attempt to stimulate such reflection, this publication, produced under the auspices of the CIS's *Religion and the Free Society* program, contains two papers by two Christian theologians who examine private enterprise from the viewpoint of their respective traditions.

Addressing the topic of business and entrepreneurship from a Protestant standpoint, Gordon Preece suggests that Christians need to rehabilitate the idea of *vocation* when it comes to thinking about entrepreneurial activity. In his view, it is not enough – and perhaps even somewhat counterproductive – for Christians to think primarily in terms of business ethics when writing and thinking about business activity. Such a focus tends to imply that there is something particularly morally hazardous about the very nature of private entrepreneurship that requires its practitioners to be given special ethical guidance. By contrast, we do not hear much discussion in either secular or religious circles of, for example, 'trade-union ethics'. Yet, as we all know, trade-union officials, or, for that matter, members of any other occupational group, are just as capable of ethically questionable acts as businesspeople. The idea of business as a vocation from God is, according to Preece, a much richer and positive way for Christians to think about business activity. To this end, Preece explores the Bible as well as the writings of a wide variety of Protestant thinkers, illustrating that they provide a sound basis for the reestablishment of what he calls a 'Protestant entrepreneurial ethic'.

Samuel Gregg examines entrepreneurship from the perspective of Catholic social teaching, and attempts to deepen its vision and understanding of business activity via a dialogue with the Austrian school of economics. Having outlined the general Austrian understanding of the nature of entrepreneurship, Gregg demonstrates that the Austrian school's grounding of entrepreneurship in the praxeology of human action chimes particularly well with Catholic teaching about the nature of human acts and the acquisition of virtue. He then brings to light the fact that much medieval and early modern Catholic reflection on economic life generally had a very positive view of business activity. This assessment, he argues, has gradually re-emerged in Catholic social teaching in the latter half of the twentieth century, not least because of John Paul II's sophisticated analysis of the nature of the human act, human work, and the right of private economic initiative. Gregg concludes, however, by suggesting that there remains much for Catholic scholars to do in this area if they are to think more constructively about entrepreneurial activity. Interestingly, he stresses that this will involve viewing such activity as a vocation, a point also underlined by Preece.

This is only one of the common emphases emerging from these two papers written from the perspective of two different Christian traditions. Others include the need for Christians to be more cognisant of the *history* of Christian thought about economic issues, the study of which should cause some contemporary Christians to rethink their less-than-positive view of business activity. Entrepreneurs and business practitioners are certainly deeply involved in the world of Mammon. This book, however, illustrates that, at its best, such activity is a powerful and authentic expression of what Christians, Jews, and Muslims believe to be man's nature as the *imago Dei* and man's obedience to Yahweh's command, expressed in the Book of Genesis, to 'be fruitful, multiply, fill the earth, and subdue it' (Genesis 1:28).

Greg Lindsay
Executive Director
The Centre for Independent Studies

About the Authors

S amuel Gregg has an MA in political philosophy from the University of Melbourne and a DPhil in moral theology from the University of Oxford. The author of *Challenging the Modern World: Karol Wojtyła/ John Paul II and the Development of Catholic Social Teaching* (1999) as well as many articles, he is Resident Scholar at the Centre for Independent Studies and Director of its Religion and the Free Society programme.

G ordon Preece has an MA in history from the University of Sydney, a ThL from Moore Theological College, a BD from the University of London, a MScSoc from the University of New South Wales, and a PhD in theology from Fuller Theological Seminary, Pasadena, USA. He lectures at Ridley College, University of Melbourne, and is Director of its Centre of Applied Christian Ethics. Rev. Preece is the author of numerous articles as well as three books, including *The Viability of the Vocation Tradition* (1998) and *Changing Work Values: A Christian Response* (1995). He is an ordained member of the Anglican Church of Australia.

1.

Business as a Calling and Profession:

Towards a Protestant Entrepreneurial Ethic

Gordon Preece

I. Introduction[1]

A prominent Protestant businessman, now retired, told me recently how he had once spoken about business at an Anglican church only to be told by two young men that a Christian could not possibly be engaged in such a sordid activity. They would not be alone. A large number of Protestant Christians today would be uneasy with the claim that business can be an avenue of one's Christian calling. Given the bad press that many transnational business corporations get, and some deserve, this is understandable. Yet, I will argue, it is ultimately misguided, representing an amnesia about one of Protestantism's great distinctives, the doctrine of the universal calling or vocation of all believers, in whatever biblically lawful places of service they find themselves.

For some, this dis-ease about business is justified rationally, drawing on a range of sources – Scripture, Aristotle, Anabaptism or Marx. Some others simply have a gut reaction that business is only about filthy lucre. 'Others may say that the pastors, teachers, physicians and social workers. . . . may have callings but not the managers, marketeers, financiers and accountants' (Lambert 1997: 1). They are concerned that the holy title of 'calling' may dignify a dirty business or perhaps offer a blank cheque of Christian endorsement to an area of murky moral ambiguity. But are the former occupations intrinsically better than the latter? The aim of this paper is to retrieve the Protestant doctrine of vocation and the related concept of profession as a way of both affirming business but also as a critical resource for guiding contemporary business in a more ethical and accountable direction.

Some may be sceptical of the relevance of religion in general, and Protestantism in particular, to a global business environment. Yet Samuel Huntington's *The Clash of Civilizations and the Remaking of World Order* (1998) argues that the major world conflicts today are increasingly religiously and culturally based – witness Indonesia.

---

[1] Lake Lambert kindly made his thesis available to me which has been of inestimable help with this paper.

It behoves us therefore to address this dimension in economic affairs as we move out of our parochial Western secularism into regions where religion matters much more publicly. As social ethicist Denis McCann writes:

> If you plan to work for a multinational corporation, for example, you are likely to encounter a multiculturalism that raises theological issues heretofore reserved only for high-level inter-religious dialogue. The religious terrain upon which multinational corporations operate is no longer the Protestant franchise that Weber described. . . . The increasingly prominent multinationals based in East Asia are based on neo-Confucian values. . . . How can Americans [or Australians] evaluate the corporate culture in such firms without understanding the religious values operative in them? Conversely, how can Americans [or Australians] compete with them without understanding their own, still largely unacknowledged, religious assumptions? (McCann 1995: 3)

The Protestant doctrine of vocation is unacknowledged due to secularisation and also increasing work mobility making the notion of one vocation for life relatively rare (Preece 1998: 268-269; Volf 1991: 105-109). This has left business people somewhat rudderless in navigating the occasionally treacherous waters of transnational commerce. Despite some noble attempts, contemporary Christianity has failed to cultivate fully a climate of discernment about how contemporary economics and business works in practice and how they should work in precept. Re-acknowledging and revising the historically well-pedigreed Protestant notion of calling would be a better way forward than contemporary new age quests for a spirituality of work.

Many agree. Historian, Denis de Rougement, claims that 'the great social and cultural maladies of the modern age all have this one common characteristic: they deny personal vocation' (1963: 37). Robert Bellah's team of sociologists (1986: 287-288, cf. 66ff.) advocates 'reappropriation of the idea of vocation' concerned with the public good rather than personal advancement as a way of bridging the private and public spheres and developing more meaningful work and 'a more democratic' and less utilitarian economy (1992: 106). Developmental psychologist, James W. Fowler, sees vocation as central to an integrated view of human life stages (1984; 1987: chps. 2-3). Professional ethics specialist, William May, regards the idea of vocation as 'more inclusive than that of a profession and more communally oriented than the modern idea of a career' (1988: 2).

There is empirical support for these advocates of the importance of vocation. Surveys indicate that those who report having a sense of calling experience more satisfaction and meaning in their work and try harder (Wuthnow 1994: 73). Further, this is not just a Christian phenomenon. TV serials about good cops, lawyers, doctors and their ethical struggles imply 'that the best life is that led under the star of vocation' (Carroll 1998: 21). A secular health-care editor sums it up well: 'I think most of us are looking for a calling, not a job. . . . Jobs are not big enough for people. It's not just the assembly line worker whose job is too small for his spirit' (Terkel 1977: 421-24).

The loss of a sense of vocation is a key reason why many scholars, ministers and lay people describe the difficulty of making the Sunday-Monday connection. It is especially difficult for business people because of the suspicion that their work is unspiritual and cannot be a calling (Diehl 1976: v, vi; Lambert 1997: 2; Preece 1995: 3-5). This reinforces the privatisation of faith and morality – Christian ethics are for the bedroom, not the boardroom.

This second-class status is despite the fact that business executives are even more active than the already high average of church activity in the US than all other professions (Stackhouse 1995: 7). Many there, and in Australia, feel marginalised from their churches, their workaday concerns either banished or trivialised when pastors or denominational representatives speak ignorantly on economics. In one recent case, a preacher unfairly bit the business hand that partly fed his social welfare organisation. Some Church welfare groups, with a vested Constantinian dependence upon the state, have a perceived bias against business.

A further reason for the alienation of business people from some churches is that academics, who are often used by pastors for social understanding, are often uncomfortable with the business world.

But as the novelist V.S. Naipaul points out, those whose calling is to write, to publish or perish, would perish without a complex network of interdependence on a range of callings including business.

> I was given the ambition to write books. . . . But books are not created just in the mind. Books are physical objects. To write them you need a certain kind of sensibility; you need a language, a certain gift of language. . . . [but to] get your name on the spine of the created physical object, you need a vast apparatus outside yourself. You need publishers, editors, designers, printers, binders, booksellers, critics, newspapers, and magazines and television where the critics can say what they think of the book; and of course, buyers and readers. . . . [I]t is easy to take it for granted. . . . to think of writing only in its personal. . . . aspect. . . . [B]ut the published book, when it starts to live, speaks of the cooperation of a particular kind of society. . . . [with] a certain degree of commercial organization (Naipaul 1991: 22).

Having set the scene, my plan is: first, to partially define Protestantism; second, to engage with its basic text, the Bible, about economics and business; third, to sketch the Early and Medieval Church's exaltation of contemplation as a vocation over action or commerce; fourth, to trace the development of the distinctive Protestant view of universal vocation; fifth, to ask how to apply notions of vocation and profession to contemporary business; sixth, to relate the Protestant notions of vocation and profession to the corporation; seventh, to ask about the distinctive purpose or vocation of business corporations; eighth, to offer some conclusions. In short, I will argue for the contemporary contribution of the notion of business as a vocation and profession to an entrepreneurial ethic for a global marketplace.

II. Defining Protestantism

A standard definition of Protestantism is 'the system of Christian faith and practice based on the acceptance of the principles of the

Reformation. The term is derived from the protestation of the reforming members of the Diet of Speyer (1529) against the Catholic majority' (Cross and Livingstone 1974: 1135). Thus a negative definition of Protestantism is simply 'not Roman Catholic' (Garrison 1952: 9, 12). Protestantism's negativity to Catholicism was based, 'across the spectrum', on the critical 'conviction that in the earlier history of Christianity something had gone wrong'. 'A critical process and commitment to scriptural accountability' available to the priesthood of all believers led to 'a fundamental scepticism' and subordination of Church tradition.

This doubt is expressed classically in the New Testament, which says that all of God's people should be kings or priests or prophets or charismatics. Different 'Protestant' criticisms have made this point with different degrees of radicality, but all have in some way or another sought to redefine or relocate the prerogative of the priesthood [or papal magisterium] in moral discernment. . . . by virtue of a critical principle of appeal to the sources (Yoder 1984: 15-17).

The notion of protest is still basic to Protestantism, no matter how conservative and conformed to the world it has become in some forms. 'When it comes to making their spiritual and moral lives whole. . . . modern Protestants do not bide their time, surrendering to tradition, any more than their sixteenth-century counterparts did' (Ozment 1992: xiii).

III. The Bible, Wealth, and Business

Protestants are thus people of the Book. We will therefore look at the Bible to see what light it casts on business. For those who are reluctant, Max Stackhouse rightly pronounces that:

> Anyone concerned with modern economic life who has not wrestled with the biblical materials that have shaped our society is not yet fully professional. The manager, union organizer, trustee, lawyer, engineer, professor of economics, or member of the clergy who attempts to speak of business matters does not know whence certain of the deepest

patterns in modern business derive unless that person knows something about Scripture (Stackhouse 1995: 37).

Differences Between Biblical 'Wealth' and Contemporary Productive Capital

There is a common assumption, backed by biblical texts, that engagement in wealth creation is not a valid biblical calling. Yet we should beware of anachronistically reading back our economic structures into Scripture. Biblical anthropologist, Bruce J. Malina, notes how biblical and Mediterranean economies did not exist in themselves but were embedded in kinship and political contexts of belonging. Wealth and poverty, including the prohibition of interest for loans to Israelites (e.g., Deut. 23:19-20), were evaluated by whether they brought honour or shame in kinship and political terms. 'Cultural criteria of the day had the word "poor" pointing to the socially impotent, while the label "rich" or "wealthy" [including the merchant in the Hellenistic and Roman periods] attached to the greedy and avaricious' depriving the poor of due honour. . . . and contentment with readily available necessities of life' (Malina 1995: 90-93).

Economists likewise note that both wealth and capital, as notably exercised by Hebrew kings, were seen as devoted to conspicuous consumption, war or religious edifice complexes.

> Conspicuously absent from these means of utilizing wealth is its application for a purpose. . . . constitutive of capitalism . . . not as an end in itself, but as a means of gathering more wealth. The closest analogue to this in ancient kingdoms, is the employment of military or religious or regal institutions and equipages, not merely as symbols of power and prestige desired for their own sakes but as instruments for military, religious, or dynastic expansion (Heilbroner 1985: 34-35).

Jim Halteman, an Anabaptist economist, one of the more anti-capitalist Protestant groups, notes that:

> Pre-capitalist societies had no understanding of the economic-growth-and-prosperity mentality of the twentieth-century capitalist. . . . [B]iblical writers had little

if any understanding of productive capital as a form of wealth. Instead, wealth was viewed as hoarded future consumption that contributed nothing to future production. . . . [A] no-growth subsistence orientation. . . leads naturally to strong admonitions against accumulated wealth and to a concentrated focus on income distribution questions rather than production questions. . . . Not until A.D. 1000 did capital inventions and innovative processes begin to expand production in ways that caused some to think of continued growth as a possibility (Halteman 1988: 55-58).

Reformed theologian John Schnieder (1994: 24) agrees. Ancient economic systems failed to create freedom and wealth for the majority. They were top-down, trickle-up, autocratic systems, profitable for a few. Poverty was seen as something always with us. The idea of arming people to eliminate it, rather than merely giving alms to alleviate it, is relatively recent. The new political order of democracy and economic order of capitalism gave many people unprecedented wealth and control of their circumstances.

However, as Halteman (1988: 62-63) wisely notes:

It would be inappropriate to downplay the sharp condemnation of wealth in Scripture simply because productive wealth is now more common than hoarded wealth. The danger of idolatry is present in all times. However. . . . it is inappropriate to condemn a wealthy business person today by using the anti-wealth passages of Scripture if his wealth is accumulated in productive tools for socially desirable output and he successfully resists the temptations of being rich. . . . Sadly, believers have not carefully distinguished hoarded productive wealth in a no-growth steady state economy and productive wealth in a capital-oriented economy. . . . so business people today are criticized by many believers who use Scripture as if they lived in the first-century world.

In reaction, the Christian business person often seeks scriptural texts, usually in Proverbs, to show that Scripture is not anti-wealth. In its extreme forms, this becomes an individualistic 'health and wealth' gospel which brings about a consequent reaction from South American and other liberation theologians. Though understandable, given their contexts, neither approach understands the whole biblical context in a balanced way.

Genesis: God's Great Risk on Human Dominion Over Creation

To understand the whole biblical perspective on business and wealth it is best to work our way through its main forms of literature, law, prophets, wisdom, gospels and epistles from beginning to end. In Genesis, we find God depicted not as an impersonal Aristotelian first cause or Prime Mover but in personal, relational, almost entrepreneurial terms as 'The God Who Risks'.

> God's activity does not unfold according to some heavenly blueprint whereby all goes according to plan. God is involved in an historical project, not an eternal plan. The project does not proceed in a smooth, monolithic way, but takes surprising twists and turns because the divine-human relationship involves a genuine give-and-take dynamic for both humanity and God. . . . God establishes the relationship in such a way that he risks the possibility of rejection (Sanders 1998: 88-89).

Most of all, God risks by making a distinct creation and a free humanity to rule it, each with its own identity. Genesis 1 depicts God's delight in the sheer abundance and extravagance of creation and creativity and His invitation to humanity to share in it. As Tolkien says, we are 'sub-creators', made in God's image to have responsible dominion over the earth, to develop and 'keep' it with care (Genesis 1:26-28). Humanity's place in creation is one of 'dominion with delight'.

In Genesis, the image of God and dominion is not merely ascribed to kings as in most of the ancient world, but is democratised. All have dominion. Without this democratised dominion, modern technologies or economies simply could not be conceived. We would still live in fear of the forest spirits. The dominion or cultural mandate unleashes the universal creativity and initiative of every man and woman. It is the original *magna carta* of human liberation, as

Nicholas Wolterstorff (1983: chp. III) shows liberation theologians.

However, this God-given sense of initiative is soon directed away from creation in a futile quest for infinite, divine prerogatives (Genesis 3:1-7). This Promethean pretension put creation and humanity at enmity. Work and birth both became literally hard labour (Genesis 3:16-19). And yet the mandate to develop the earth is renewed, though modified, through Noah after the great flood (Genesis 9:1-17). Humans were made to be enterprising, entrepreneurial beings, even if fallen.

The Exodus and Jubilee Laws of Economic Liberation

Unfortunately, unlike Israel, Egyptian rulers believed that dominion was only theirs. Like most ancient civilisations, theirs was built on the backs of (in this case Hebrew) slaves. God's demonstration of dominion over the Nile and the Red Sea in liberating Israel from Egypt ended their exploitation and opened up the possibility of true dominion over creation again in an Edenic 'land flowing with milk and honey' (Exodus 3:8 NRSV).

Israel's laws are extrapolations of the Exodus, the enshrining of freedom and democratic dominion into the very fabric of its social and economic life. However, forms of economic domination over others' means of production or land soon arose. But the Jubilee laws (Leviticus 25) on which the Jubilee 2000 campaign for remission of Third World debt is based, were developed to counter it. While neither socialistic nor capitalistic, their vision of justice, individual liberty, irrevocable property rights and banking, lending and productivity has more in common with democratic capitalism, at its best, than proposed alternatives.

The Jubilee was not a 'communist manifesto' of redistribution 'to each according to his need'. Rather, the Jubilee in fact 'stresses and safeguards the function of private property as an *incentive* to industrious energy. . . . Lv 25 implies that the independent small property-owner is the backbone of a representative government' (North 1954: 163). As John Hartley says (1992: 447-448):

> The Jubilee manifesto has not been lost on the pages of a forgotten OT book. It has had a leavening effect on social

thought in the West, as the inscription of the words of v10, 'proclaim liberty throughout the land', on the Liberty Bell attests. This legislation has contributed to the Western idea that every family has a right to own property. The view of land ownership herein, however, is revolutionary. . . . . It promotes responsible work that attends ownership of property, and at the same time it promotes responsible brotherhood of all Yahweh's people.

God liberated Israel into a life of extravagant productivity. He was the true fertility God, the Creator God, but if they forgot God and their less fortunate fellows in their new found prosperity, and worshipped wealth and other gods, it would soon vanish (Deuteronomy 8:7-20). This happened with their exile into landlessness for forgetting God as the source of their salvation and its outward sacrament – land and material blessing.

Prophets and Profits

There is a common contemporary assumption that Israel's prophets were against profits. Numerous texts, especially in Amos, thunder God's wrath at the rich who 'sell. . . . the needy for a pair of sandals' (Amos 6:6-7). The rich Israelites' oppression of the poor was the equivalent of the war crimes of their neighbours (against a kind of Genevan Convention or natural law) whose condemnation they warmly approved (Amos 1 and 2).

Yet Amos condemns not delight in the good things of life in themselves, but rather the people's narcissism and callous indifference to the poor (Amos 6:1-7). Instead of practising Exodus principles of material and social liberation and solidarity, they adopted an Egyptian way of life and will be judged and exiled. However, God's people will return, refined, to unprecedented fertility and abundance (Amos 9) and the liberty and justice of the Jubilee laws will be proclaimed (Isaiah 61:1-2).

Proverbial Wisdom

As mentioned earlier, perhaps the most business friendly biblical traditions are found in Proverbs. Proverbs provides a strong middle-class ethic of family loyalty, hard work, and honesty grounded in respectful fear of God. Wealth is good, though tempting, while poverty is bad and tempting. A middle way is best. 'Give me neither poverty nor riches. . . . or I shall be full, and deny you, and say, "Who is the Lord?" or I shall be poor and steal, and profane the name of the Lord my God' (Proverbs 30:8-9 NRSV).

It is dangerous, however, to develop a rigid retributive scheme which turns generally descriptive proverbs into prescriptions claiming that honesty and hard work always pay. Job's friends pushed this utilitarian line, claiming that Job's suffering was due to lack of integrity. Satan claimed that Job only feared God for what he could get. Job, however, held to his integrity and was finally rewarded: firstly, with a vision of God's transcendence and creative and spontaneous delight in the diversity of creation with all of its inherent riskiness and freedom to flout rigid laws; finally, with much more than he lost before (Job 38-42). Job, in the end, puts character before cash, just as God had bet that he would (Job 1:6-12). This is all part of the Bible's much more holistic, relational view of God's covenant with humanity than a rigid utilitarian contract.

Jesus and Wealth

There is a common romantic picture of Jesus as a rustic Galilean peasant, possibly even a Che Guevera or Zealot-type revolutionary that simply does not fit the evidence. Jesus' birth was not only attended by the poor shepherds, but also by the well-off astrologers from the East who brought expensive gifts (Matthew 2:1-12). Jesus belonged to a small business family of builders (Mark 6:3), part of the Galilean middle-class of skilled workers (Hengel 1963: 26-27). While not rich, he probably had ample work on the big construction projects at the sophisticated Greco-Roman city of Sepphorus a few kilometres away (Batey 1992). Jesus' middle classness probably enabled him to move inclusively across classes, to identify with the poor crowds and the rich tax collectors alike.

John Schneider (1994: 112-113) highlights the implications of the locus of Jesus' incarnation being unappreciated by many contemporary ethicists and church leaders:

> Jesus' chosen place in his society as a tradesman reflects a certain *goodness* on property, on creative, productive work and on the sort of personhood that goes with it. The commercial system is thus, in a way, redeemed through his economic person. . . . The New Adam himself worked at a productive trade within the economic system of Israel in the Roman Empire. He was a builder and a businessman, and this was apparently part of what expressed his perfection as a human being.

The common view that Christians must stand somehow outside the system of 'sinful' economic structures, while taking sin and the West's complicity in such structures seriously, downplays the fact that we cannot – and Jesus did not – simply slip out of the system. The Creator God still sustains and blesses the world in which Jesus had a relatively privileged position. 'He benefited from the stability of peace, legal order, good road systems, stimulated cash flow and building projects. . . . that improved standards in his own region'. But the structures of Roman power also included totalitarianism, militarism, slavery, extortionate taxation and occasional genocide.

> Because Jesus was a true human being who lived and worked within that economic system, it was simply impossible that he did not profit from very great structural evils. And so far as we know He did nothing directly to change them. . . . This seems to have been an outrage to his more puritanical contemporaries, who thought him careless about his contacts with people such as Roman soldiers, tax collectors and others who typified cultural godlessness. . . . The principle of 'guilt by implication' is so relentless, rigid and unforgiving, then, that not even Jesus can pass its tests for goodness (Schneider 1994: 115).

This discredits such a rigid rule as a criterion for Christian economic and vocational life.

Having earthed Jesus economically in the Galilean construction industry, it is nonetheless important to stress that He primarily constructed God's Kingdom and His primary business was God's business (Luke 2:49). This relativises all earthly activities, entrepreneurial or socially activist, even revolutionary, in the light of what Karl Barth calls 'the revolution of God' against all unrighteousness (1961: 544-545). Business is good, but it is not God.

Jesus' First Followers

There is a widespread assumption that Jesus' followers were mainly poor. Though Jesus announced a Jubilee, upon the Jewish and Gentile poor (Luke 4:18), his followers came from all walks of life. The first group, the disciples, included middle-class fishermen with their own boats and servants – one of the biggest businesses on the lake – fish being the basic source of protein. Levi was a wealthy tax collector (Luke 5:29). To follow Jesus, they left behind relative wealth and security.

The second group followed Jesus but not on the road. They supported him and his disciples from their relatively well-off position (Hengel 1963: 27). These include 'Peter's mother-in-law, Lazarus and his sisters Mary and Martha, wealthy men like Joseph of Arimathea, and the wealthy women "who provided for them [Jesus and his disciples] out of their resources" ' (Luke 8:3).

A third group, the crowds, included a range of people from poor to rich. The latter, tax collectors like Zaccheus (Luke 19) and prostitutes, were people of high status inconsistency – high in economic but low in social status. This opened them up to Jesus. Jesus took both the relatively privileged and underprivileged and created a rich and vibrant Jubilee community out of them (Mark 10:28-31).

But if Jesus did not condemn the material world as evil, like 'a radioactive landscape', how should we interpret His life of poverty and His blessings upon the poor and woes to the wealthy (Luke 6:20-27)? As George Forell says: 'Jesus, who had some standing in the Christian tradition, did not exactly end as president of the Chamber of Commerce of Jerusalem' (1973: 85). The traditional answers are insufficient. On the one hand, Catholics distinguish between the counsels of perfection for an elite who take vocational vows (of poverty, chastity and obedience) and ordinary Christians in 'secular' jobs with families to support. However, Jesus' commands are to be taught to *all* baptised disciples (Matthew 28:20). On the other hand, Protestants tend to limit Jesus' poverty to the unique circumstances of his mission. His poverty is 'not for us to imitate, but to venerate, and more loosely to emulate'. They see Gospel ethics as descriptive then, more than prescriptive now.

Liberation theologians working with the poor rightly question these means of voiding Jesus's demands. Yet they catch themselves in a paradox if the poor are blessed and yet Jesus comes to bring them out of their socio-economic poverty or 'blessing'. If poverty is so blessed, why take them out of it? (Schneider 1994: 129-30).

An alternative reading sees Jesus as the true human who fulfils the dominion mandate to rule creation, now gone wrong, with delight and compassion. He miraculously calms storms, feeds the hungry, heals blind eyes. He spends much of His time feasting. In fact, Jesus was crucified for the way He ate and who He ate with. He was condemned as 'a glutton and a drunkard, a friend of tax collectors and "sinners" '(Luke 7:34 NRSV). While Jesus challenged His followers to disinvest in this world's ways and invest their resources and talents in His reign, we often confuse the means – disinvestment and self-denial – with the end, extravagant experience of God's abundance for all (Luke 18:28-30).

Jesus does not deny the principle of 'profit', but radically relocates it in relation to one's whole life and His kingdom. 'What does it profit them if they gain the whole world, but lose or forfeit themselves?' (Luke 9:25 NRSV). His reign is the best risk, the best investment, the best bet. The calling to be disciples of Jesus in the business world involves great tension between these different principles of profit, but no more than in any other area of life.

> In sum, Jesus called his followers to lives of redemptive sacrifice and celebrative delight. Perhaps the outer ring of followers, including especially Zaccheus, is the best 'type' for professional people. . . . These 'righteous rich' committed their possessions and their positions in the world to the work of redemption in the fullest sense. . . . A poverty of spirit animated their delight, and this proved itself in free and effective actions of good will toward the poor and the powerless (Schneider 1994: 143-44).

IV. Contemplation over Action: The Early and Medieval Church

Greek Dualism's Disparagement of Business

Having surveyed the relatively positive biblical view of material work and clarified the difference between status wealth then and productive wealth now, it is important to examine some of the Greek philosophical and historical factors disparaging work and business which Protestant notions of vocation reacted against.

Lewis Mumford argues that the Greek city-states failed to 'moralize trade' by bringing it within the realm of 'legitimate human enterprise' (Graham, 1987: 116). Trade was 'essentially suspicious, if not downright perverted' (Malina 1995: 93 citing Aristotle 1932: III, 12-20, 1257a-58a). As Aristotle said:

> Any occupation, art, science which makes the body or soul or mind of the freeman less fit for the practice or exercise of virtue, is vulgar. Wherefore, we call all those arts vulgar which tend to deform the body and likewise all paid employment, for they absorb and degrade the mind. Anybody who does anything for pay is by nature not truly a free person (Forell 1973: 84-85).

From the second century B.C., after Aristotle's student Alexander the Great conquered the Mediterranean world, Greek influence penetrated Israel. In the Greek world, material work was a necessity not fit for free men, who engaged in politics and philosophy – only slaves worked. Greek influence is seen in the apocryphal wisdom book, Ecclesiasticus. While more respectful of trades than the Greeks or the Egyptian *Satire on the Trades*, it still exalts the scribe/philosopher over the tradesperson. Though workers are needed to 'tend to the fabric of this world' (38:34), they have no leisure or freedom, unlike scribes, to contemplate wisdom, but must focus on their narrow task. The merchant especially 'can hardly remain without fault' (26:29) for 'between buying and selling sin is wedged' (27:2). In sum, business is bad, work is necessary and neutral to good, and contemplation is better because it is free.

This unbiblical Greek priority of contemplation over action and commerce foreshadows the Early and Medieval Church's exaltation of contemplative Mary over active Martha (Luke 10:38-42). It was adopted and adapted by St. Augustine, whose doctrine of the Church was central to Medieval Christendom, and whose doctrine of grace was central to the Protestant Reformers. Augustine helped establish the three key pillars of a Christian view of economic life:

• the goodness of creation, work, productivity, and private property;
• a utilitarian distinction between use and enjoyment, meeting needs not wants; and
• poverty is on a higher spiritual plane than relative riches (Schneider 1994: 32). This is why only those who took the monastic vow of poverty were said to have a calling.

The Restriction of Calling to Monks

New Testament calling language refers: firstly, to God's universal call to conversion and/or corresponding conduct (Ephesians 1:18, 4:1; II Peter 1:10); secondly, to particular social roles in the classic Protestant vocation text, 1 Cor. 7:20, 'stay in the calling [social role] in which you were called [converted]' (KJV). This second particular sense was largely ignored in the Early Church in favour of the first general sense of discipleship.

With the easing of persecution, however, Emperor Constantine's conversion (312 A.D.), infant baptism and rising nominalism, calling came firstly to refer to those leaving the world of ordinary work and wealth for monastic poverty, prayer, and perfection.

The seizure of the title *vocatio* by monasticism prevented for a long time in the West the development of a proper religious evaluation of secular occupations and made it impossible for the word *vocatio* to become customary for them. I Cor 7:20, just as in the East, remained essentially without influence in this direction in spite of the fact that as early as Tertullian the translation of *klesis* by *vocatio* is to be found. There is no passage in the writings of the early Fathers where *vocatio* means anything like occupation (Holl 1958: 136-137).

Parallel with this is the fact that Clement of Alexandria (150-215 A.D.) appears to be the sole Church Father taking a positive view of entrepreneurialism and capital (Gordon 1989: 87).

Secondly, the slow theological development of the universal doctrine of vocation was due partly to the Early Church's economic environment being less differentiated, and having limited status and occupational distinctions compared to the later Middle Ages and modernity. Thus, there was 'no stimulus which might eventually give birth to the idea of a stable, well arranged system of "callings" and the division of labor' which became the vocational ideal for several centuries (Troeltsch 1992: 121-122).

Thirdly, most monastic rules mixed prayer, reading and manual labour, in that order, best balanced in Saint Benedict's rule of the sixth century, which remained a minority position through the Middle Ages, but whose restricted approval of labour Protestants may have generalised (Sommerville 1992: 72). Later, Brother Lawrence's Carmelite spirituality was expressed through work in *The Practice of the Presence of God* (1692/1975) as he polished pots and pans and scrubbed the floors of the monastery kitchen. But while work was seen as worship or prayer – *labore et orare* – the former was a mere material or disciplinary means to intellectual and spiritual ends: to eradicate self. The more mundane the work, the easier to turn the mind to prayer (*Rule of Benedict* chp. 57; Holl 1958: 136-37). In one extreme form, monks made baskets and then unmade them.

This strictly timed monastic discipline, however, led to the invention of clocks to govern the monastic hours of prayer and work. In the eleventh and twelfth centuries, monastic discipline and asceticism began to be universalised and secularised, setting in place 'the basic structures of centralized and rationalized control that have characterized Western society ever since' (Ovitt 1987: 196). This aided the development of the Protestant Work Ethic and modern business (Sommerville 1992: 81; Weber 1958: 118-119, 158, 174).

Fourth, a step towards a more balanced biblical and ultimately Protestant view of work was taken by Walter Hilton (1988: 229-35), a fourteenth century Augustinian canon. He wrote letters to an English layman, important in commercial and political life, who had a profound spiritual experience and wanted to enter a contemplative community, abandoning family and business. Hilton wisely counselled a third way, a 'mixed life' combining the activity of Martha with the reflectiveness of Mary. However, none of these Medieval thinkers broke with the priority of the contemplative life as thoroughly as Martin Luther (1483-1546).

V. Protestant Vocationalisation of Work and its Later Secularisation

Luther and Calvin's Expansion of Calling or Vocation

The great Protestant contribution toward the practice of business has been its universalising of the notion of calling. From our secularised perspective that equates vocation with a job, it is difficult to understand the revolution that Luther achieved in taking a term monopolised by the spiritual elite of monks and applying it to 'secular' work. Luther's translation of the Greek *klesis* in 1 Cor 7:17, 20, 24 and elsewhere by the German *Beruf* (from *rufen* - to call) led to the popular European use of the term vocation for daily work (Luther *WA* 12: 122-23; Hart 1995: 43-45; Holl 1958: 145; Weber 1958: 207).

Such secular work included not just one's 'job' but the domestic/ economic, political and ecclesiastical work of all believers (*LW* 37: 364, 41: 177; 3: 217). A whole range of relational responsibilities were seen as avenues through which people love and serve God and others (*LW* 46: 246; Althaus 1972: 36; Schwarz 1996: 6-9; Wingren 1957: 5). Luther was the first to regard all works, not just religious works, and thus all vocations (except overtly sinful ones) as fundamentally equal (Holl 1958: 142-43), just as all believers are equally priests and saints before God (Hart 1995: 37-40).

Despite, however, this positive and revolutionary step, there is some debate about how medieval or modern Luther's attitude to business was. Heiko Oberman (1992: 87, 84) observes that:

> Luther was born into a modern world. At the family table, he heard the story of the budding mining industry and became aware of the problems of the entrepreneur. Thus, early in life, he learned abut the impact of early capitalism in practice and not just in theory. . . . Luther's later treatment of the far-reaching influence of large

companies was knowledgeable, critical and surprisingly unacademic. The Luther family experienced all the vicissitudes of a small business.

Luther was, however, perplexed by 'the emerging mercantile system and the values of the middle-class' (Schneider 1994: 23-24). Lake Lambert finds Luther dismissive of Christian involvement in trading companies:

> This is why no one need ask how he may in good conscience be a member of a trading company. My only advice is this: Get out; they will not change. If the trading companies are to stay, right and honesty must perish; if right and honesty are to stay, the trading companies must perish (*LW* 45, 272).

With his pivotal role in vocation's doctrinal development, it is troubling that Luther had such a harsh view of the business of his day, and there was certainly dishonesty and injustice as there is with all social activity in any age. But the real question is whether Luther understood the businesses and economics which he was condemning, and the answer appears to be in the negative. Relying on the economics which he had learned from Aristotle, Luther had no way to understand the growing international trade and commerce of his day, nor could he make sense of the large companies which arose independent of agriculture and the guilds. Luther, unfortunately, yoked his new vision of vocation to an old view of commerce. But while regrettable, Luther's lack of economic expertise should not prevent the use of his development of vocation and the application of the Reformation tradition of vocation to work in modern business. He certainly was not the first (or last) to grasp a valid theological notion and to lack the social analysis to apply it accurately (Lambert 1997: 79-80).

The only way to reconcile this contradiction about Luther's business attitude and acumen is to admit that he is a man of contradictions, not least, despite Oberman, between his radical theology and conservative sociology, illustrated for instance in his Medieval condemnation of usury. Perhaps too, Luther's sympathy extended only as far as the small businesses of which he had most experience. Still, Lambert's point about the continued serviceability of Luther's doctrine of vocation stands.

Since Weber's Protestant Ethic thesis, Luther and especially Calvin have often been portrayed as forerunners of modern capitalism, but it is more true of Calvin. Both stressed the almost universal applicability of vocation to material labour as equal to 'spiritual' tasks lauded in the more elitist and dualist ideologies of Medieval Catholicism and Anabaptism. Calvin's reading of the parable of the talents (Matthew 25) in a more literal sense of economic stewardship had a liberating economic effect. Further, because Calvin could

> distinguish between lending for consumption at interest – a crime akin to murder – and lending for production and enterprise, he was able to sanction low rates of return [up to 5%] for the latter. The rule of charity in his hands was more flexible than the Aristotelian natural law which the church had inherited and wielded so clumsily for many centuries (Graham 1987: 124).

Although Geneva was only a small city and haven for many French refugees like Calvin himself, he organised the deacons to put them all, from low to high, to work, in what became a hive of entrepreneurial activity. A French aristocrat was shocked at seeing a fellow noble degraded into making buttons, illustrating the difference between 'the old French aristocracy and the new Genevan entrepreneurs'. 'Work. . . . was the great Genevan leveller' (McGrath 1990: 232-33). Professional education for youth, temporary employment, the creation of new trades in the weaving industry, and laws against gambling led to a 'peaceful revolution' or war on poverty providing the 'opportunity to rise out of impoverishment' (Buckley 1984: 12).

Calvin's stress on universal vocation not only affirmed business, but was able to hold it accountable to the common good and God's glory, unlike the Athenian antipathy to business the Church had inherited.

> Because Athens, and to a lesser extent the medieval city, considered trade outside the pale, it was left largely

unregulated and left in the control of social and religious untouchables. So when Calvin dared compare trade with the life of the godly. . . . he was, in effect, bringing the Genevan bourgeois under the influence of restraint by blessing his activity (Graham 1987: 116).

The Secularisation of Vocation

A century after Luther and Calvin, English Puritan substitutes for the Medieval, and partly Lutheran, 'Great Chain of Being' with its hierarchical and organic patterns were created. These voluntary covenants dependent on commitment to one's vocation had democratic implications, making people dependable, and opening up political callings (Walzer 1972: 198-99, 213). Along with rising economic and educational mobility, this led to greater possibilities of choice and change of vocation.

The drawback of this tide of mobility, however, was the loss of the New Testament and early Puritan distinction between general and particular vocation. William Perkins' 1603 classic, *A Treatise of the Vocations or Callings of Men* (1970), subordinated particular callings (family, citizenship, and work) to the end of a Christian's general calling to God's glory, salvation and the common good (Michaelson 1953). The later Puritans (and Deists like Benjamin Franklin) forgot this and became the prime example of Weber's Protestant Ethic thesis.

Puritan spiritual discipline and inner worldly asceticism became a secularised rationalisation of time and money during the accumulation phase of early capitalism. Vocation was equated with occupation and became a secularised end in itself (Marshall 1996: 45-49, 135 n12; Troeltsch 1992: 645-46; Weber 1958: 78, cf. 108, 181). Work became increasingly a means to:
• efficient production, profit, and potential consumption; and
• possibly proving one's predestination (McGrath 1990: 238-39) by one's worldly success and wealth. The Caller was increasingly forgotten in the calling.

The collapse of the Puritan Commonwealth after the English Civil War of the 1640s, undermined their sanctification of work and economics (Marshall 1996: 48-53). Lockean 'possessive individualism' (McPherson 1962; Marshall 1979: 73-96) reduced the remnants of John Locke's Puritan sense of calling as did the separation of technical from moral economics (Marshall 1996: 91-96). This led to the progressive privatisation and legalising of Puritan reform instincts for which their name has become famous. Capitalism thus lost much of its spiritual and moral motivation and restraint.

One who tried valiantly to resist the trend, when international trade and colonialism were expanding rapidly, was the Puritan Richard Steele (1629-1692) who wrote *The Religious Tradesman*. Steele affirms business as a calling for Christians if 'His devotion disposes him for business, and his business makes his devotion welcome' (1823: 66). Although not strong on the Reformed meaning of vocation, and simplistic in his criteria for selecting a calling ('lawfulness, suitability, advice and interest of the soul'), Steele articulated 'a vision of the calling to business which many Christians had sensed and enacted'. He provides an early model for how principles of justice and the recently rediscovered ethics of virtue can be applied to business as a vocation.

> The qualities of diligence, truth, contentment and justice were to rule the tradesman's character, and each trait included elements or rules which would guide the tradesman in his craft. Among the elements of justice were fair prices, payment of all debts, use of exact weights, parental care of all apprentices, restitution of all unlawful gains and mercy to the poor. . . . In fact, most of his rules for justice would be readily acknowledged as applicable to the modern era (Lambert 1997: 82-83).

Surprisingly, after Steele, and until the Social Gospel movement of the turn of this century, there is a deafening silence on business as vocation. John Wesley advised his Methodist followers, so named because of their methodical spiritual and economic disciplines, to 'get all you can, save all you can, give all you can'. But he foresaw the danger of this originally working-class movement thus becoming more middle-class and forgetting the original spiritual and moral motivations that forged it.

At the dawn of the Industrial Revolution with its increasing division of labour and possibilities of generating great wealth, and greater alienation at work, the religious concept of calling was ignored by the two great theorists of emerging capitalism, Adam Smith and Karl Marx, although the title of Smith's *magnum opus*, *The Wealth of Nations,* was taken from Isaiah 60.

Both Adam Smith in the eighteenth and Karl Marx in the nineteenth century believed that economics and its laws could be disembedded from the ethical and religious traditions, which, for most of human history, were thought to shape economic attitudes and behaviors. Once these laws were isolated, we could know the 'basic' causes of wealth and poverty. Smith accented the relationships of supply, demand, market, and division of labor; Marx accented the relationships of classes, the ownership of the means of production, and political power. Both saw material interests as the clue to human motivation and social history (Stackhouse 1995: 110).

In his earlier, largely forgotten book, *The Theory of Moral Sentiments* (1759/1976), Adam Smith wrote of the primary, non-material motivations of justice, benevolence and prudence of which desire for honour, respect, social advancement and wealth are subsets (Halteman 1988: 25). However, he argued in *The Wealth of Nations* that: 'It is not from the benevolence of the butcher, the brewer, or the baker that we expect our dinner, but from their regard to their own interest' (Smith 1776/1937: 14; cf. Heilbroner 1972: 52-54). But self-interest is prevented from holding society to ransom by the balancing power of the 'invisible hand' of free market competition, either a secularised natural order or divine providence.

Smith secularised the theology of vocation in terms of the prodigious productivity of the division of labour. Yet his belated warning of the alienating and de-vocationalising effects of monotonous mass production is rarely remembered: 'The understandings of the greater part of men are necessarily formed in their employments. The man whose whole life is spent in performing a few simple operations. . . . generally becomes as stupid and ignorant as it is possible for a human creature to become' (Smith 1776/1937: 734; cf. Heilbroner 1972: 66).

Sadly, without seeing work as part of a vocation to serve God and others as well as self, Smith has no answer to the problem of dehumanisation and alienation, apart from government prevention and the compensation of consumption (Volf 1991: 53-55). This reduces work to a mere means, not an end in itself. Despite its economic effectiveness, the combined influence of Smith's 'economic determinism and Darwinian (or Spencerian) "survival of the fittest" '(Graham 1987: 116) needed state regulation to moderate its impact upon the weak – as Smith foresaw. But state regulation could not provide the spiritual spontaneity and motivation that could be provided by the concept of providential calling, that is, to serve God and the common good in satisfying work. Nor could it encourage the virtues that Smith affirmed earlier.

Vocation, Advocacy, and Business Ethics

During the twentieth century, there has been some rediscovery of the significance of vocation for the laity, though emphases on political advocacy and business ethics have often overshadowed it. While arguing for the priority of vocation, I do not see it excluding a role for advocacy or business ethics.

Between the Depression and World War II, a key precursor to the World Council of Churches (WCC) was the *Faith and Work* program on the laity's vocational role in the world. This was particularly influenced by the Anglican layman, J.H. Oldham, and Archbishop William Temple (Smith 1990). Though respecting the relative empirical and policy expertise of economists, Oldham (1950) and Temple (1942: 7-10) held that religion nonetheless can subject economics to moral criteria as it had done before the rise of purely 'technical' economics in the seventeenth century. They sought bridging principles or 'middle axioms' between basic theological (God's nature and purpose), anthropological (humanity's dignity, tragedy and destiny) and social principles (freedom or respect for personality, fellowship and service), and specific economic and political policies such as unemployment policy. Such 'middle axioms' were that every willing worker should have a job and have a voice in their business or industry and know that their work serves the common good. These are distinguished from more specific policy proposals or political programs (e.g., industry policy, paid holidays etc.), which Temple relegates to an appendix to show that it has lesser authority.

Unfortunately, in their (or should I say 'our', having served on them) understandable keenness as political advocates for the poor, some Church Social Responsibilities Committees and welfare groups have forgotten Temple's important distinction. This has been particularly so since the radicalisation of the WCC (and many member churches) in the mid-sixties in its advocacy role for Third World 'liberation' against some multinational corporations and national governments. The WCC has been vocal about politics but not about the vocation of the laity as in its beginnings.

Many have questioned the dominance of advocacy over vocation. They argue that its clerical and radical agenda often forgets the Church's central task and expertise in proclaiming Christ, oversimplifies complex economic and technical questions, and obscures the role of lay vocational and ethical expertise and influence (Benne 1995; Boggs 1961; Lambert 1997: 59-61). The indirect and persuasive role of the laity living out their calling as salt, light and leaven in the working world is overshadowed by this emphasis on political power and direct action. Paul Ramsey's *Who Speaks for the Church?* calls this the 'church and society syndrome' whereby a 'social action curia' assumes expertise in every area of life (Ramsey 1967: 13, 15) often embarrassing and disenfranchising Christians with real expertise in economics and business. It implies that there is one Christian position on complex issues when they are often ambiguous and there should be liberty to disagree. Resolutionary Christianity takes over from the quiet but revolutionary doctrine of vocation.

Vocation is also somewhat marginalised by the new growth industry of business ethics. Business ethics has had some success as an antidote to the excesses of the 'Greed is good' decade of the 80s, stereotyped most starkly in Oliver Stone's film *Wall Street*. Business ethics institutes, courses, gurus and corporate codes of ethics have proliferated as universities and others have jumped on this profitable bandwagon. The danger here, however, is not clerical or political advocacy that does not recognise ambiguity, but the creation of a new group of academic experts still somewhat distanced from the laity. Further, ethics tends to be treated as another expertly imposed technique, something external, based on decisions about dilemmas and codes relatively divorced from character, identity, ethos and spirituality.

VI. Business as a Vocation/Profession in Global Corporations

Virtue and Vocation in Ecumenical and Global Context

In a global economy, historically unprecedented ethical and spiritual demands will be made upon business leaders, whose secular training or formation is rarely up to it. To sustain 'moral business', not only are external ethical codes required, but new modes: an Aristotelian and Catholic emphasis on character or virtue, not just technique or expertise; and renewed forms of Protestant vocation leading to revitalised motivation and professional formation. Catholic social philosopher, Michael Novak, argues for blending Aristotelian virtue and vocation if capitalism is to be sustained by a sense of moral order. He uses three cardinal virtues to define *Business as a Calling* (1996): creativity, community, and prudence. Novak's key virtue of creativity or 'co-creation' with God has much in common with the biblical and Reformed cultural or dominion mandate. (This is despite valid Protestant concerns that Tolkien's notion of 'sub-creation' better safeguards divine sovereignty and counters human pride [Hauerwas 1995; Preece 1995a: 219-231]). For Novak, 'Man the discoverer is made in the image of God. To be creative, to cooperate in bringing creation itself to its perfection is an important element of the human vocation. This belief. . . . was bound to lead in an evolutionary and experimental way, to the development of an economic system whose first premise is that the principal cause of wealth is human creativity' (Novak 1996: 125 and chp. 6, cf. John

Paul II 1981; Welbourn 1998). 'In the course of modern Catholic social teaching, beginning with Pope Leo XIII's encyclical *Rerum Novarum* of 1891, we can detect a distinct "reformed shift" in the Catholic estimation of the meaning and place of work in human life' (Hardy 1990: 67).

Though most highly developed in Protestantism, the notion of work and business as vocation is increasingly recognised in Catholic circles as anchored in Christian identity and profession through baptism and is able to inform discussion of business ethics with an ecumenical Christian ethos and character (Lambert 1997: 76). But is this sufficient in a global and pluralistic context?

Max Stackhouse relates the need for re-sanctifying business as a calling to the growing globalisation of the economy. He argues this in the light of:

• global population growth demanding business supply more jobs and goods and services than ever before;

• the business-technology-ecology nexus demanding that business exercise exceptional stewardship of natural resources;

• multicultural/multireligious demands made in a global market demanding greater ethical discernment;

• greater awareness of global human rights in business practice being essential; and

• the global nature of the market and increased encounters with the world's main religions making religious/ethical understanding by business essential.

In short, because business leaders are increasingly the stewards of civilization, a deeper sense of vocation or profession will be required. Fortunately, such a sense of vocation has forbears, in a range of cultures:

> Among the ancient Hebrews, with parallels in Greece, India, China, Egypt, and elsewhere, roles that required both special ability and specialized training were treated as 'callings' or 'vocations'. Persons with a 'calling' developed a disciplined life-style governed by a worldview and a value system that comprehended the

whole and guided a practical expertise, so that they could best serve God and the people in a humane context (Stackhouse 1995: 13).

Business as a Profession?

Today, despite problems with professionalism, with lawyer and other jokes poking fun at those falling short of their professional responsibilities, the jokes are made precisely because those professions have well-defined responsibilities and standards that people measure them by. Business standards are not so clear. Business people are often looked down upon as 'less ethical' by other professionals in Church, government, law, medicine, and education. Images of the sly merchant, the used car salesman, and the unscrupulous robber baron are common. A considerable number of entrepreneurs, particularly Christian business people, have a haunting suspicion that these images may be right, that they are second-class ethical citizens, engaged in a morally ambiguous activity. To cope with this uneasy conscience, I have heard some justifying their activities in terms of the 'people-work' that they do 'on the side', as if they are somehow really social workers. Fundamentally, this goes back to a Greek unease with the material creation and wealth, which, while it picks up the danger of making goods into gods, is not true to the biblical view of the fundamental goodness of the creation and the mandate to develop and care for it.

This disdain of business as a dirty business is illustrated by the regular refrain that various fields and professions such as education, law, medicine, and even religion are just becoming businesses. Business is seen by some as essentially unethical, with its own norms, outside the normal ethical norms of society or religion. Some happily confirm this, rejoicing in their autonomy, captured in the phrase 'business is business'. Yet it is unlikely that business people are personally less honest (for example) than professionals or academics. But they are in some senses less regulated by a range of vocational and professional norms. While business people understandably desire to be free from what some see as state strangulation, increasing self-regulation requires a strong vocational and professional ethic or we will revert to the survival of the fittest.

Reforming Business, Professional Associations and Education

Professionalism is suitable as a guideline for affirming and reforming business in our pluralistic societies because it is respected among a range of sub-cultures with diverse religious and ethical commitments (Sullivan 1995: 3). Professions are key mediating institutions between families and states and as such they can provide a basis for the revitalisation of contemporary community and business life. Nonetheless, the professions are increasingly in need of reform themselves.

Although there is no full agreement on a definition of profession, it tends to refer to:
• a more or less full-time, not avocational, occupation;
• based on special knowledge involving lengthy training;
• regulated by a formal credentialling process;
• dedicated to serving others rather than merely commercial profit; and
• encouraging peer group establishment of standards (Banks 1996; Stevens 1997; cf Sullivan 1995, 2).

The third criterion opens up ideas of professional initiation by oath-taking, the fourth, service or 'closet' altruism (Maxwell 1995: 6.1), and the fifth, professional codes of conduct enforced by a covenantally bound group (Sullivan 1995: 46). The new knowledge economy encourages professionals to major only on the second criteria of specialised technical knowledge (Sullivan 1995: 105-107). But the growth of the service economy balances the high-tech with high-touch (Naisbitt 1982) leading to an outward looking service ethic even if only for economic necessity's sake (Wuthnow 1996: 213-214).

The last criterion of professional association has changed with the corporatisation of society. Simultaneous with the increasing importance of technical expertise has been the rise of organisational or corporate professionals at the expense of the more traditional 'free professionals' organised into professional associations (e.g., the AMA). Today, however, 'most professionals work in government or corporate bureaucracies. . . . The corporation, rather than the professional association becomes the professional's primary source of communal identity. A blinkered vision of technical expertise and efficiency to the exclusion of social concerns often results. 'This has led. . . . the Left to demand greater state control of the professions, and. . . . the Right to seek market control and the end of what they see as monopolistic professional associations' (Lambert 1997: 138-139).

With the collapse of state socialism in Eastern Europe, corporate downsizing, the expansion of capitalism in the Third World, and the globalisation of economic life, imaginative new strategies for global corporate accountability and discernment are needed. The 'standard Christian approach' described earlier, has been to use the nation-state to go over corporations' heads. This is increasingly difficult for three reasons:

• we live in a post-Christendom context where the Church no longer has a privileged position;

• it is often impossible in a global context, where, as Daniel Bell said, many problems are both too big and too small for the nation state (cited by Giddens 1998); and

• small government and the private provision of services is increasingly practised.

In this context, 'instead of a political theology, a vocational [and professional] theology may be the best theological lens to view the business corporation' so that it can adopt 'the same intermediary and community building role which the professional association once did' (Lambert 1997: 2-5, 138-139). Given the above factors and the increasingly pervasive influence of business in the global economy and a whole range of key institutions, a deepening sense of business as a profession and vocation is vital.

Where will the resources for such a re-evaluation of business as a profession and its key institution, the corporation, come from? William Sullivan (1995: 220) advocates:

• reworking liberal ideas of free choice and personal dignity toward cultivating personal and social virtues that value the public as well as private good; and

• revitalising Christian ideas of vocation and covenant, that go beyond a career-oriented and contractual approach to professional life, to one centred more on long-term vocational service of, and covenantal commitment (cf. May 1983) to, the welfare of people and institutions.

If enough business professionals and corporations meet this challenge, they could provide models for the workforce generally. Given the high levels of responsibility and risk that new information technologies entail, and the extension of entrepreneurial initiative so that some speak of everyone in an organisation being an 'intrapreneur', professionalism's best features must be extended to all modern work (Sullivan 1995: 124-125).

Many professionals would recoil with horror at this suggestion. Yet the social commentator, Christopher Lasch (1991: 483-84, 500), rightly questions their arrogant belief that other occupations involving commercial interests, manual work, or less formal education, are inferior or inherently corrupt. Such professional elitism also loses sight of the original democratic origins of the modern movement towards professionalism and its background in the Protestant notion of the priesthood and vocation of *all* believers. A view that business managers cannot be professionals is in danger of becoming a new 'priesthood of the professionals' (Nichol 1980) that leaves an ignorant and ill-equipped laity to face the challenges of the new millennium. Instead:

> It is time for business, the belated profession, to come into its own. . . . This requires, of course, the professionalization of modern business precisely in the sense that it develops among business leaders the moral and spiritual capacity to guide their increasing expertise and emerging institutions with clarity about and commitment to the well-being of the commonwealth of nations (Stackhouse 1995: 19).

'Moral and spiritual capacity' was something that a process of education and initiation imbued in the professions. Business leaders have lagged behind in the process of professional education, but are rapidly catching up. Yet despite the proliferation of business schools and business ethics courses, many still teach a modern (Enlightenment) distinction between facts and values while the post-modern humanities are saturated with value-laden political assumptions. An extension of the process of professionalisation is needed in business education, but one that has something to profess, going beyond secular theories of success and enlightened self-interest to build the ethical foundation of the business corporation on the Protestant doctrine of vocation and of business enterprise as stewardship.

VII. Vocational/Professional Vows, Corporate Codes and Missions

Vocational and Professional Initiation, Priorities and Direction

A vocational/professional lens provides a much broader view of business. If one is called, one is answerable firstly to God and God's global and local people. This is the general calling of all Christians. It is the first place where identity and accountability lies. Secondly, particular callings include not only a job, but domestic calling and calling to citizenship, which may have increasingly global and ecological connotations.

To avoid vocation lapsing into a merely subjective internal process, it is important to link it with the more public and corporate notion of a professional vow. The most basic professional vow for Christians is that of baptism as the fount of Christian identity. This response to the general calling to all Christians can be linked to a particular call to a specific profession whose clear and respected oaths of office were modelled originally on the ordained ministry. Is there any such equivalent for what business professionals recognise as obligatory standards in their business dealings?

The closest we come to such professional standards is the corporate code and mission statement. As Lambert notes: 'Today, ancient creeds of the classic professions like the doctors' Hippocratic Oath may be replaced by oath-like mission statements such as the Johnson and Johnson Credo. Not all these standards will be upheld, but they articulate a new meaning for professionalism in an "employee society".' This enables like nothing else 'the realization of management as a vocation in the classic sense, and these creeds will also clarify and sustain the traditional Christian meaning of *professio.*'

Most of the other aspects of professionalism are already present. 'A synthesis between technical knowledge and the social sciences has developed a discrete body of knowledge known as business management', but technical knowledge is necessary, not sufficient, to qualify as a profession. Professions must be judged by their ethical ends, not mere technical means or even their outward observance of corporate creeds and codes. A focus on purely deontological, duty or act based ethics likewise can foster a limited and literal 'letter of the law' approach that misses the spirit and goal. '[M]anagement cannot be a true profession. . . . unless it not only has a code and an organized group taking responsibility for standards but also makes a commitment to responsibilities and social goods beyond the corporation's economic ends, excellences of technique, and the means required to reach them' (Lambert 1997: 138-141).

Professional management responsibilities, goals and the quality of products and services will have to be weighed to see if they confirm or contradict God's call and a Christian's baptismal identity. The context of the modern corporation with its institutional history, structure and culture will also have to be evaluated to see if its purpose is ethical or not (Lambert 1997: 112).

Corporate Purposes or Callings

Our modern personalised readings of the callings of prophets and kings in the Old Testament and Jesus and the apostles in the New often ignores their more corporate dimensions as representatives of the general calling or vocation of God's people (Lambert 1997: 12). Max Stackhouse picks up this more biblical corporate perspective and sees the corporation's purpose or *telos* as its vocation, adapting the term from its more common contemporary individualistic use (1987: 133-34). 'In more ambiguous terms which might be taken from religious or from military terminology, others speak of a corporation's mission' embodied in mission statements (Lambert 1997: 142; cf. Pattison 1997: chps. 2, 4). One church with which I am familiar encourages its members to compare Jesus's mission with the mission statements of the institutions in which they work, a very useful exercise which confirms that the two can be related, both positively and negatively.

While it sounds strange to secularised ears to hear biblical notions of corporate calling connected to modern corporations, the latter's roots are, in fact, primarily ecclesiastical. They are found in 'covenantal and stewardly motifs, canon law, and monastic practices which created a structure and ethos that facilitated the modern corporation's emergence'.

> [F]irst Jews and then Christians actually rejected Roman forms of corporate association because they required approval by the state. According to Christian teaching [and canon law], any group of persons which had the requisite structure and [divine] purpose. . . . constituted a corporation, without the special permission of a higher authority. The 'higher authority' which Jews and Christians recognized was the God who allowed the state and created the entire world. Under organizations corporately formed in accord with divine purposes were legitimate without the permission of the state. The state was not the model for the corporate form of the Church as much as covenantal motifs from the Old Testament and Pauline imagery of the Church as Christ's body (His corpus) in the New Testament (Lambert 1997: 64).

Later, monasticism developed economic production outside the household and stewardly concerns for the right use of property, tools and time. 'A combination of democratic vision, covenantal values, and rationality eventually prompted the expansion of the corporate form and structure for commercial purposes and as a new form of economic stewardship'. With the advent of Protestantism, the idea of vocation was universalised beyond the monastery and the work ethic linked with notions of covenant to produce the modern corporation (Stackhouse 1987: 126-27, cf. Herman 1995, 514-520).

The corporation is the modern form of the economic order's institutional expression previously obscured by its subordination to and integration into the *oikos* [house], *polis* [city state], or some combination of them. It is arguably the predominant and most important today. Theologically, it may be a sign of God's preserving love in that it sustains the common life in this historical epoch (Lambert 1997: 153).

Corporations as Covenantal Associations

Corporations are covenantal associations. 'Covenant is. . . . the community-ordering side of vocation' (Stackhouse 1987: 27). Most corporations are voluntary, covenantal and mediating associations between the state and family. Sociologist, Talcott Parsons (1978: 202-203), sees voluntary associations as relatively new social forms 'with roots in the Reformation and its understanding of the New Testament as a new covenant'. James Luther Adams likewise argues that since early Christianity 'rejected civil religion, allowed voluntary membership and transcended ethnic divisions', Christianity was in fact the first global corporation (1986: 175). Reformed (and some Roman Catholic) congregationalism and covenantal social forms also provided the basis for the extension of trust in non-state and non-familial forms such as small businesses and corporations. This is essential to covenantal (more personal) and even economic contractual (more functional) relations as Francis Fukuyama shows in his book *Trust*:

> [A]lthough property rights and other modern economic institutions were necessary for the creation of modern businesses, we are often unaware that the latter rest on a bedrock of social and cultural habits that are too often taken for granted. Modern institutions are a necessary but not a sufficient condition for modern prosperity and the social well-being that it undergirds; they have to be combined with certain traditional social and ethical habits if they are to work properly (1995: 150).

The necessity for such relations nurtured in mediating institutions has been highlighted by the burgeoning movement to re-establish civil society which has both left (Cox 1995; Sennett 1998) and right forms (Fukuyama 1995; Novak 1996: 135-138). A society that relies merely on legally coercive contracts and consumer carrots rather than a range of covenantal trust relationships in voluntary associations incurs increasing legal costs for enforcement and undermines the very freedom that is the genius of capitalism. It also undercuts the committed families, character and delayed gratification (definitive of psychological maturity) necessary to maintain a work ethic, long term vision and democracy (Berger 1983: chps 7-8; Sennett 1998). Vocation is currently being voided by short-term contractual approaches to work contracts.

The Purpose (s) of Corporations

What then is the business corporation's reason for being or its calling? The business professional in a corporation cannot discover their vocational calling divorced from the corporation's calling. As David Smith says, among Reformed Protestants 'the professional is called not to accept but to reform or change the world according to the ideals of his or her calling. . . . [T]he professional is called to a special responsibility for society as a whole. S/he is a public official with leadership responsibilities – physicians should work for public health, lawyers for civil rights, etc.' What is the proper correlative responsibility for business? (Smith 1988 cited in Stackhouse 1995: 15).

A commonly quoted answer is Milton Friedman's – that the purpose of business is purely to maximise profits:

> The proximate purpose of business everywhere is to increase wealth, and wherever business does not do that it fails. But what is viewed as wealth, who is to have access and control of it, how capital is used, what criteria are used to decide how it ought to be used, and what goods and services are most treasured vary from culture to culture.

And, one might add, from religion to religion. However, Friedman refuses to go beyond the proximate purpose to the ultimate or even penultimate. He holds that businesses cannot bear social responsibility or a social conscience: 'Only people can have responsibilities. A corporation is an artificial person and. . . . may have artificial responsibilities' through its CEO. 'He has direct responsibility to his employers. That responsibility is to conduct the business in accordance with their desires, which generally will be to make as much money as possible while conforming to the basic rules of the society, both those embodied in law and those embodied in ethical custom' (Friedman 1970: 32-33).

Friedman is right that CEOs have no right or responsibility to use owners' money for charity or moral crusades without permission. He is also right about the artificiality of corporations, because a corporation cannot literally have intentions like a person. 'But this does not mean that anything goes, morally speaking, in business. . . Organisations such as business firms, football clubs, churches, and political parties are "*quasi-moral systems*".' We rightly treat them *as if* they have moral responsibilities. Business firms do not constitute 'morality havens'.

> In general there are moral side-constraints on how individuals use their property, and on what principals can legitimately expect their agents to do on their behalf. . . . [I]t *would* be morally illegitimate for shareholders to demand that firms act unjustly. . . . on their behalf. . . . The fundamental defect in pure stockholder theories [like Friedman's] is that they attempt to wall commerce off from the rest of life. . . . Pure stockholder theorists are committed to saying *either* that business firms are not linked to individuals and other organisations by gratitude, professional responsibility, promise-giving etc, *or else* that they are, but these relations never give rise to moral liabilities of firms, beyond those generated by the basic imperative to maximise the interests of shareholders within the law. Neither alternative is attractive. The former is a manifest sociological falsehood. The latter. . . . stands out as ad hoc, arbitrary, and therefore implausible (Langtry 1993: 9-15).

Further, as Stackhouse observes:

> 'Profit' is surely too limited a vision of management's ends. Profit is, in fact, only an indicator of whether or not the company is doing well in the short term. And every culture and every religion approves of profit *if it does not in itself become the chief end of life, displacing all other ends, and if it contributes to the well-being of the commonwealth*. The larger task of business depends on its long-term ability to create

the kinds and quantities of wealth that serve humanity
and honor all that is holy (Stackhouse 1995: 28).

Theologically, Reformed Protestants have a wonderful guide to
the question of our chief end in the Westminster Shorter Catechism's
answer 'to enjoy God and glorify Him forever'. Anything less is
ultimately unprofitable and idolatrous. Sociologically and ethically,
Friedman also begs the big question of what should compose the
'laws' and 'ethical customs' that limit profits. Ironically, 'constraints
are necessary in order for there to be a "free market". Lands that
have not developed legal systems that simultaneously control
corruption and encourage business remain underdeveloped, as one
can see when one compares Eastern and Western Europe, North
and South Korea. . . . or the Philippines and Japan' (Stackhouse
1995: 28, 18).

If we ask after a corporation's purpose or vocation, we find
that not only is it most obviously a legal entity, but that it also
has limited liability, in recognition of a certain social contribution
and risk. The concept of social stakeholders, not just
stockholders, is built into this. Managers are trustees or stewards,
not only for the owners of capital, but also for society and its
social capital, and for employees who share in some sense of
'commonwealth'. Thus corporations exist not only to make profits
but also to serve society by:
• producing products, goods and services which meet needs
and wants and without which they will disappear; and
• providing work – part of the creation commission to develop and
care for the earth (Lambert 1997: 147-150).

From a different part of the political and philosophical spectrum
comes another view that still sees business as basically about profits.
Alasdair MacIntyre is an ex-Marxist, now Catholic moral
philosopher who has set the contemporary agenda for ethical
thinking with his seminal book *After Virtue* (1981). MacIntyre argues
that the Enlightenment abandoned the virtue tradition of Aristotle
and Aquinas based on an ethical end or purpose for human nature
in favour of our individual pursuit of happiness. Since then modern
morality has become mere manipulation of others to endorse our
personal preferences (emotivism). For MacIntyre, the manager is
typical of modern society in using techniques and means to maintain

a willing and efficient workforce to keep profits up. MacIntyre shares with Ecclesiasticus, Aristotle, Luther and Marx, the assumption that acquisition is the sole purpose of commerce. He sees institutions generally, and business especially, as primarily interested in the 'external goods' of power, status and especially wealth.

MacIntyre's negative assessment of business has bad examples like Union Carbide at Bhopal or the Exxon Valdez to back it up. Yet there are also positive examples like Johnson and Johnson or Herman Miller which show that business corporations can be a context for practising virtues and can have ends beyond profit. In fact, MacIntyre reluctantly admits that the virtues of social practices need institutions to sustain them. However, he shares Aristotle's preference for politics as a school or social practice for justly integrating the various goods of life, both internal (virtues) like courage, and external such as prosperity for the sake of the common good (1981:175-183).

Yet this begs the question whether that co-ordinating or justice function cannot also be exercised by business if we separate it from MacIntyre's nostalgia for the Greek *polis* and Aristotle's assumption that acquisitiveness is somehow definitive of business? McCann and Brownsberger (1990) answer affirmatively. MacIntyre could appreciate business as a social practice if he recognised:

• that acquisitiveness and the tunnel vision of the bottom line is not the monopoly of business, but common in government also; and

• the possibility of virtue being nurtured in voluntary associations such as corporations. In principle, MacIntyre should be open to this as he notes the way that virtues change over time with different social settings. The modern business corporation is merely a further part of this development (McCann and Brownsberger 1990: 512-513) which may be replaced by some future form.

In contrast to both Friedman and MacIntyre, Peter Drucker's management classic, *The Practice of Management* (1973), argues that the purpose of business is to 'create or serve a customer' – to form 'an association of economic betterment'. Trust and mutual benefit are the internal goods or ethical excellences which serve the goal of economic community. The external good of making a profit is a secondary, but necessary means to this end (McCann and

Brownsberger 1990: 509-510) in order to compensate risk and attract capital without which the internal goods or virtues could not be gained (Drucker 1974: 374). Even Aristotle recognised this (1984: 1.1099). For Drucker, acquisition is not solely definitive of business; association is as well.

Management theorist, Peter Anthony (1984), supports Drucker – managers in practice have to operate as members of a community. Leading Calvinist businessman, Max DePree, former chairman of Herman Miller Co., also backs Drucker. For De Pree, profit is like breathing – we breathe to live, not live to breathe (1979: 9, 11). Companies make profits as social entities serving communities. If profits are an end in themselves and not a means to providing some service then surely most businesses would be better off simply investing in the futures markets.

Ethically, the professional manager should serve or vow loyalty to the purpose or mission of the organisation, not primarily the organisation itself or the making of profit at all costs. Business managers need to remind corporations what their primary purpose is. As Stackhouse says: 'If a university becomes a political party, or a psychiatric center, if a corporation becomes a military camp or a charity organization, if a church becomes a museum or a court of law, it has betrayed its central vocation' (1987: 25).

The 'idiosyncratic purpose' or vocation of an organisation can often be evaluated in terms of the mission statement of the organisation. For instance, Johnson and Johnson's code – 'We are responsible to the communities in which we live and to the world community as well' – was famously practised with their costly but ultimately profitable withdrawal of the drug Tylenol after samples were tampered with (Lambert 1997: chp. 5). This demonstrated that principles and profits can mix. A further local and personal example comes from when I was on the board of WorkVentures, a church-based entrepreneurial job creation and training project in Sydney's Eastern Suburbs. We were challenged by some staff to aim our project at the whole Sydney area. However, our mission was to serve a local community with multiple impact and particularly to serve our stakeholders in that community – Aboriginals, migrants, long term unemployed, etc. – and we stuck to it (Preece 1995: 124, chp.

3). That was our corporate vocation and the sum of many individual vocations. Such a synergy between corporate and personal or professional vocation is far from impossible, though there are often tensions between them.

A key tension, of course, is produced by the pressure to produce short-term profits for stockholders including CEOs who are often large stockholders, through the sacrifice of stakeholder interests, for example by downsizing employees. The overseas evidence indicates that these policies are not even in the prudential or long-term self-interest of such corporations. Chronic downsizers' share prices suffer long-term falls. Further, ethical policies can pay. Many of the most ethical companies regularly feature in lists of the most financially healthy. Another way forward is for stakeholders to increasingly become stockholders as in Herman Miller Co. or as corporations like Telstra and other corporations become partly directly owned by more average Australian stockholders and by superannuation funds on their behalf. The question is, will these people hold business accountable to its broader goals and stakeholders or merely pursue short-term gain? In the end, we all, at least all stockholders, bear some responsibility if business fails to live up to its higher calling.

VIII. Conclusion

A distinctively, though not exclusively, Protestant approach to business as a calling or profession is one that is based strongly on the Bible as its primary principle of 'protest' or judgement and on the Protestant Reformers' view of universal vocation. The Bible has a positive view of material reality and of humanity's role in developing and caring for it although well aware of the ambiguity that attends our fallen state. This provides a base for a positive view of business as a calling. Despite the appearance of biblical condemnations of wealth, these are more about conspicuous consumption and the pursuit of honour, not the use of productive wealth which sustenance economies were largely unfamiliar with.

Unfortunately, the Early and Medieval Church was influenced by the more negative Greek view of material reality which exalted the contemplative life over the active life, and particularly commerce. Thus only monks were described as called or having a vocation until Luther universalised vocation, despite his suspicious of trading companies. Calvin and the Puritans had a more positive view of business as a vocation, but the Puritans' demise led to the secularisation of vocation.

In the twentieth century, attempts to revive the concept of vocation have had some success although it has been sometimes sidelined by churches focusing on political advocacy or business ethics. With the contemporary global dominance of business, yet still considerable suspicion of it, the time is ripe to sanctify business as a calling and profession, not only to affirm it, but to hold it accountable to professional standards. For business to be classed as a profession, however, it was necessary to demonstrate that, contrary to Aristotle and his contemporary followers, profit or acquisition while necessary, is not the primary purpose of business corporations, but rather service and association. A Christian professional called to serve God in a corporation and pledged to its mission and code should uphold its mission to serve the community even against the corporation, but ultimately judge it by their primary calling and profession as a Christian.

In this light, Walter Rauschenbusch's prayer for a group of businesspeople is an appropriate way to end:

> May thy Spirit, O God, which is ceaselessly pleading within us, prevail at last to bring our business life under Christ's law of service, so that all who share in the processes of factory and trade may grow up into that high consciousness of a divine calling which blesses those who are the free servants of God and the people (Rauschenbusch 1910: 64).

Abbreviations

KJV   *King James Version of the Holy Bible.*

LW   *Luther's Works.* Vols. 1-30, ed. J. Pelikan; Vols. 31-
           55, ed. H. T. Lehmann. Concordia and Muhlenberg/
           Fortress Press, Philadelphia/St.Louis, 1955-1976.

NRSV   *The Holy Bible: New Revised Standard Version* , Collins,
           Glasgow, 1989.

Bibliography

Adams, J.L. 1986, 'The Social Import of the Professions' and 'The Voluntary Principle' in *Voluntary Associations,* ed. J. Ronald Engel, Exploration Press, Chicago.

Althaus, P. 1972, *The Ethics of Martin Luther*, tr. R.C. Schulz, Fortress Press, Philadelphia.

Anthony, P.D. 1984, 'The Metamorphosis of Management, from Villain to Hero', in *Towards Information Society,* ed. R.C. Barquin and G.P. Mead, Etsevner Publications, N. Holland.

Aristotle. 1932, *Politics*, Harvard University Press, Cambridge.

——. 1984, *Nicomachean Ethics*, in *The Complete Works of Aristotle,* ed. J. Barnes, Princeton University Press, Princeton.

Banks, R.J. 1996, 'Professional Integrity', *Ridley College Centre of Applied Christian Ethics Newsletter* I/1.

Barth, K. 1961, *Church Dogmatics* III/4, ed. G. W. Bromiley and T. F. Torrance, T. and T. Clark, Edinburgh.

Batey, R.A. 1992, *Jesus and the Forgotten City,* Baker, Grand Rapids.

Bellah, R. et.al. 1986, *Habits of the Heart: Individualism and Commitment in American Life*, Harper and Row, New York.

——. 1992, *The Good Society*, Vintage Books, New York.

Benne, R. 1995, *The Paradoxical Vision*, Fortress Press, Minneapolis.

Boggs, W.H. 1961, *All Ye Who Labor,* John Knox Press, Richmond.

Berger, B., and P.L. Berger. 1983, *The War over the Family: Capturing the Middle Ground*, Anchor/Doubleday, New York.

Bouwsma, W.J. 1988, *John Calvin: A Sixteenth Century Portrait*, Oxford University Press, New York.

Brother Lawrence, 1692/1975, *The Practice of the Presence of God*, Baker, Grand Rapids.

Buckley J. 1984, 'Calvin's View of Work', *Radix* (January/February): 8-12, 28.

Carroll, J. 1998, *Ego and Soul: The Modern West in Search of Meaning*, HarperCollins, Sydney.

Cox, E. 1995, *A Truly Civil Society,* ABC, Sydney.

Cross F.L., and E.A. Livingstone, eds. 1974, *Oxford Dictionary of the Christian Church*, Oxford University Press, Oxford.

DePree, M. 1979, 'The Process of Work: Is This a Brother-Keeping Business?' *Reformed Journal* 29: 9-11.

Rougement, D. de. 1963, *The Christian Opportunity*, Holt, Rinehart and Winston, New York.

Diehl, W. E. 1976, *God and Real Life*, Fortress Press, Philadelphia.

——. 1991, *The Monday Connection: A Spirituality of Competence, Affirmation, and Support in the Workplace,* Harper and Row, San Francisco.

Drucker, P. 1973,*The Practice of Management*, Harper and Row, New York.

——. 1974, *Management: Tasks, Responsibilities, Practices,* Harper and Row, New York.

Forell, G. 1973, *The Proclamation of the Gospel in a Pluralistic World*, Fortress Press, Philadelphia.

Fowler, J. 1984, *Becoming Adult, Becoming Christian*, Harper and Row, New York.

——. 1987, *Faith Development and Pastoral Care,* Fortress Press, Philadelphia.

Friedman, M. 1970, 'The Social Responsibility of Business is to Increase its Profits', *New York Times Magazine,* 13 September: 32-33.

Fukuyama F. 1992, *The End of History and the Last Man,* Hamish Hamilton, London.

——. 1995, *Trust: The Social Virtues and the Creation of Prosperity,* Hamish Hamilton, London.

Garrison, W.E. 1952, *A Protestant Manifesto,* Abingdon, New York.

Giddens, A. 1998, *Reith Lectures*, BBC Radio, London.

Gordon, B. 1989, *The Economic Problem in Biblical and Patristic Thought,* E.J. Brill, Leiden.

Graham, W.F. 1987, *The Constructive Revolutionary: John Calvin and His Socio-Economic Impact,* Michigan State University Press, Chicago.

Guinness, O. 1998, *The Call,* Word Books, Nashville.

Halteman, J. 1988, *Market Capitalism and Christianity*, Baker, Grand Rapids.

Hardy, L. 1990, *The Fabric of This World: Inquiries into Calling, Career Choice and the Design of Human Work*, Eerdmans, Grand Rapids.

Hart, I. 1995, 'The Teaching of Luther and Calvin about Ordinary Work: 1. Martin Luther (1483-1546)', *Evangelical Quarterly* 67 (1): 35-52

Hartley, J. 1992, *Leviticus. Word Biblical Commentary,* Word Books, Dallas.

Hauerwas, S. 1995, "Work as Co-Creation – A Remarkably Bad Idea', in *In Good Company: The Church as Polis*, University of Notre Dame Press, Notre Dame: 110-122.

Heiges, D. 1984, *The Christian's Calling* (rev. ed.), Fortress Press, Philadelphia.

Heilbroner, R.L. 1972, *The Worldly Philosophers*, Harper Touchstone, New York.

——. 1985, *The Nature and Logic of Capitalism,* W.W. Norton, New York.

Hengel, M. 1963, *Property and Riches in the Early Church*, tr. J. Bowden, Fortress Press, Philadelphia.

Herman, S.W. 1995, 'The Potential for Building Covenants in Business Corporations', in *On Moral Business: Classical and Contemporary Resources for Ethics in Economic Life*, ed. M. Stackhouse et.al., Eerdmans, Grand Rapids.

Hilton, W. 1988, 'Epistle on the Mixed Life', in *The Law of Love*: *English Spirituality in the Age of Wycliff*, tr. and ed. D. Jeffrey, Eerdmans, Grand Rapids.

Holl, K. 1958, 'History of the Word Vocation (Beruf)', tr. H. F. Peacock, *Review and Expositor* 55.

——. 1959, *The Cultural Significance of the Reformation,* Living Age Books, New York.

Huntington S. 1998, *The Clash of Civilizations and the Remaking of World Order,* Pocket Books, London.

John Paul II. 1981, *Laborem Exercens*, Catholic Truth Society, London.

Kreider C. 1980, *The Christian Entrepreneur*, Herald Press, Scottdale.

Lambert, L. 1997, *Called to Business: Management as a Profession of Faith*, Princeton Theological Seminary Ph.D. dissertation ms. Available from UMI, Ann Arbor.

Langtry, B. 1993, 'Stockholder Theories of the Social Responsibilities of Business', Department of Philosophy Preprint Series, University of Melbourne.

Lasch, C. 1991, *The True and Only Heaven: Progress and its Critics,* W.W. Norton, New York.

Luther, M. 1955-1976, *Luther's Works*, Vols. 1-30, ed. J. Pelikan; Vols. 31-55, ed. H.T. Lehmann, Concordia and Muhlenberg/ Fortress Press, Philadelphia/St.Louis.

McCann, D.P. 1995, 'A Word to the Reader', in *On Moral Business*, ed. M. Stackhouse et.al., Eerdmans, Grand Rapids.

McCann D.P., and M.L. Brownsberger. 1990, 'Management as a Social Practice', *Annual of the Society of Christian Ethics*: 223-245.

McGrath. A. 1990, *A Life of John Calvin*, Basil Blackwell, Oxford.

MacIntyre, A. 1981, *After Virtue: A Study in Moral Theory*, University of Notre Dame Press, Notre Dame.

McPherson, C.B. 1962, *The Political Theory of Possessive Individualism: Hobbes to Locke,* Clarendon Press, Oxford.

Malina, B.J. 1995 'Wealth and Poverty in the New Testament and its World', *Interpretation* 41 (4): 354-366.

Marshall, G. 1982, *In Search of the Spirit of Capitalism: An Essay on Max Weber's Protestant Ethic Thesis*, Columbia University Press, New York.

Marshall, P. 1979, 'John Locke: Between God and Mammon', *Canadian Journal of Political Science* 12: 73-96.

——. 1986, 'The Shape of Modern Work', in *Work in Canada,* ed. J.F. Peters, Wilfred Laurier University, Waterloo, Interdisciplinary Research Seminar Occasional Paper 4: 5-24.

——. 1996, *A Kind of Life Imposed on Man: Vocation and Social Order from Tyndale to Locke,* University of Toronto Press, Toronto.

Maxwell, M. 1995, 'Human Solidarity', unpublished MS.

May, W.F. 1983, *The Physician's Covenant*, Westminster, Philadelphia.
——. 1988, 'Vocation, Career, and Profession,' unpublished paper.
Meeks, W. 1983, *The First Urban Christians: The Social World of the Apostle Paul*, Yale University Press, New Haven.
Michaelson, R.S. 1953, 'Changes in the Puritan Concept of Calling or Vocation', *The New England Quarterly* 26.
Naipaul, V.S. 1991, 'Our Universal Civilization', *New York Review of Books*, 31 January: 22.
Naisbitt, J. 1982, *Megatrends*, Warner Books, New York.
Nelson, R.H. 1991, *Reaching for Heaven on Earth: The Theological Meaning of Economics,* Littlefield Adams, Lanham.
Nichol, I.G. 1980, 'Vocation and the People of God', *Scottish Journal of Theology* 33 (4): 361-373.
North, R. 1954, *The Sociology of the Biblical Jubilee*, Pontifical Biblical Institute, Rome.
Novak, M. 1996, *Business as a Calling: Work and the Examined Life*, Free Press, New York.
Oberman, H. 1992, *Luther: Man Between God and the Devil,* Doubleday, New York.
Oldham, J.H. 1950, *Work in Modern Society*, Geneva.
Ovitt, G. 1987, *The Restoration of Perfection: Labor and Technology in Medieval Culture*, Rutgers University Press, New Brunswick/ London.
Ozment, S. 1992, *Protestants: The Birth of a Revolution,* Fontana, London.
Parsons, T. 1978, *Action Theory and the Human Condition,* Free Press, New York.
Pattison, S. 1997, *The Faith of the Managers: When Management Becomes Religion*, Cassell, London.
Perkins, W. 1970, 'A Treatise of the Vocations or Callings of Men', in *The Work of William Perkins*, ed. and intro. I. Breward, Courtenay Press, Appleford: 441-476.
Preece, G.R. 1995a, *Changing Work Values: A Christian Response*, Acorn, Melbourne.
——. 1995b, 'Everyday Spirituality: Connecting Sunday and Monday', *Zadok Paper* S76.
——. 1998, *The Viability of the Vocation Tradition in Trinitarian and Reformed Perspective*, Edwin Mellen, Lewiston.

Ramsey, P. 1967, *Who Speaks for the Church?* Abingdon, Nashville.

Rauschenbusch, W. 1910, *For God and the People: Prayers for the Social Awakening*, Pilgrim Press, Boston.

Redekop, C.W. ed. 1996, *Entrepreneurs in the Faith Community: Profiles of Mennonites in Business,* Herald Press, Scottdale.

Sanders, J. 1998, *The God Who Risks: A Theology of Providence,* InterVarsity Press, Downers Grove.

Schneider, J. 1994, *Godly Materialism: Rethinking Money and Possessions*, InterVarsity Press, Downers Grove.

Schwarz, H. 1996, 'Martin Luther's Understanding of Vocation in the Light of Today's Problems', *Lutheran Theological Journal* 30 (1): 6-9.

Sennett R. 1998, *The Corrosion of Character*, W.W. Norton, New York.

Smith, A. 1759/1976, *The Theory of Moral Sentiments,* Liberty Classics, Indianapolis.

——. 1776/1937, *An Inquiry Into the Nature and Causes of the Wealth of Nations,* Random House, New York.

Smith, D.H. 1988, 'Called to Profess: Religious and Secular Theories of Vocation', Annual Meeting of the Society of Christian Ethics.

Smith G.W. 1990, 'The Theology of Work in the Postwar Period', MA thesis, University of Sydney.

Sommerville, C.J. 1992, *Secularization in Early Modern England: From Religious Culture to Religious Faith*, Oxford University Press, New York/Oxford.

Stackhouse, M.L. 1987, *Public Theology and Political Economy*, Eerdmans, Grand Rapids.

——. et. al., ed. 1995, *On Moral Business: Classical and Contemporary Resources for Ethics in Economic Life*, Eerdmans, Grand Rapids.

Steele, R. 1823, *The Religious Tradesman*, Francis S. Wiggins, Trenton.

Stevens, R.P. 1997, 'Professions/Professionalism', in *The Complete Book of Everyday Life*, ed. R. Banks and R.P. Stevens, InterVarsity Press, Downers Grove.

Sullivan, W.M. 1995, *Work and Integrity: The Crisis and Promise of Professionalism in America,* Harper Business, New York.

Temple, W. 1942, *Christianity and the Social Order*, Penguin, Middlesex.

Terkel, S. 1977, *Working* (rev. ed.), Peregrine, London.

Troeltsch, E. 1912/1986, *Protestantism and Progress: The Significance of Protestantism for the Rise of the Modern World*, Fortress Press, Philadelphia.

——. 1992, *The Social Teachings of the Christian Churches,* 2 vols., tr. O. Wyon, Westminster/John Knox Press, Louisville.

Tropman, J.E. 1998, 'Catholic and Protestant Ethics: Competing or Complementary Conceptions of the Public Good', in *The Consuming Passion: Christianity and the Consumer Culture*, ed. R. Clapp, InterVarsity Press, Downers Grove.

Volf, M. 1991, *Work in the Spirit*, Oxford University Press, New York.

Walzer, M. 1972, *The Revolution of the Saints: A Study of the Origins of Radical Politics*, Athenaeum, New York.

Weber, M. 1930/1958, *The Protestant Ethic and the Spirit of Capitalism*, tr. T. Parsons, Unwin, London.

Welbourn, D. 1998, 'Co-creation with God', Parts 1-3, *Faith in Business* 2: 1-3.

Wingren, G. 1957, *Luther on Vocation*, Muhlenberg Press, Philadelphia.

Wolterstorff, N. 1983, *Until Justice and Peace Embrace*, Eerdmans, Grand Rapids.

Wuthnow, 1994, *God and Mammon in America,* Free Press, New York.

——. 1996, *Poor Richard's Principle,* Princeton University Press, Princeton.

Yoder, J.H. 1984, *The Priestly Kingdom*, University of Notre Dame Press, Notre Dame.

2.

The Rediscovery of Entrepreneurship

Developments in the Catholic Tradition

Samuel Gregg

[A man] on his way abroad summoned his servants and entrusted his property to them. To one he gave five talents, to another two, and to a third one; each in proportion to his ability. Then he set out. The man who received the five talents promptly went and traded with them and made five more. The man who had received two made two more in the same way. But the man who received one went off and dug a hole in the ground and hid his Master's money. Now after a long time, the Master of those servants came back and went through his accounts with them. The man who had received the five talents came forward bringing five more. 'Sir', he said, 'You entrusted me with five talents; here are five more that I have made'. His Master said to him, 'Well done, good and faithful servant; you have shown that you can be faithful in small things, I will trust you with greater; come and share in your Master's happiness'. Next the man with two talents came forward. 'Sir', he said, 'You entrusted me with two talents; here are two more that I have made'. His Master said to him, 'Well done, good and faithful servant; you have shown that you can be faithful in small things, I will trust you with greater; come and share in your Master's happiness'. Last came forward the man who had the one talent. 'Sir', he said, 'I heard you were a hard man, reaping where you have not sown and gathering where you have not scattered; so I was afraid, and I went off and hid your talent in the ground. Here it is; it was yours, you have it back'. But his Master answered him, 'You wicked and lazy servant! So you knew that I reap where I have not sown and gather what I have not scattered? Well then, you should have deposited my money with the bankers, and on my return I would have recovered my capital with interest. So now, take the talent from him and give it to the man who has the five talents. For to everyone who has will be given more, and he will have more than enough; but from the man who has not, even what he has will be taken away. As for this good-for-nothing servant, throw him out into the dark, where there will be weeping and grinding of teeth

(Matthew 25:1-30).

I. Introduction[1]

In light of the parable of the talents, one would expect that Christianity would find it relatively easy to come to terms with the forces of economic creativity. For while the theme of good stewardship resonates through this parable, Christ also specifies that preservation is not enough: creativity is *mandatory*.

[1] The author wishes to thank Professor Ian Harper, Rafe Champion, Barry Maley, and Dr. Gordon Preece for comments and criticisms.

Nonetheless, it has taken the Catholic Church, at least during the twentieth century, quite some time to recognise the critical role played by entrepreneurship in economic life. Oswald von Nell-Breuning, S.J., the distinguished philosopher-economist who helped draft Pope Pius XI's 1931 social encyclical *Quadragesimo Anno*, stressed this on several occasions. In this regard, he singled out the Second Vatican Council's 1965 Pastoral Constitution on the Church in the Modern World *Gaudium et Spes* for special attention. Given the Council's praise of the dynamism of modern economies, Nell-Breuning found it 'all the more odd that the key-figure in this economy, *the entrepreneur*, is not mentioned in any way' (Nell-Breuning 1969: 291). Certainly, Nell-Breuning noted, businesses are made up of people who contribute labour or capital. Nonetheless, he insisted that one could not ignore the fact that '[w]ithout question, *intellectus* comes first, that is. . . . initiative and enterprise' (Nell-Breuning 1969: 299).

Lack of attention to the entrepreneur, however, has not only manifested itself in Catholic social teaching. For much of this century, there has been a tendency on the part of some economists to underplay the entrepreneur's role. Israel Kirzner points out that 'as economic theory became more sophisticated, as marginal analysis and market equilibrium theory came to be more carefully and more fully articulated, the entrepreneur receded more and more from theoretical view' (Kirzner 1985: 3). Harvey Leibenstein agrees, suggesting that it is one of the 'curious aspects of the relationship of neo-classical theory to economic development' that 'in the conventional theory, entrepreneurs, as they are usually perceived, play almost no role' (Leibenstein 1978: 9). Put another way, entrepreneurship is a phenomenon that did not fit easily into the equilibrium mould associated with the then-dominant neo-classical economic paradigm. Consequently, some economists found it easier to ignore entrepreneurship and focus on discovering 'deeper', more 'orderly' economic regularities. As Malcolm Fisher remarks: 'Mathematical model builders, whether constructors of general equilibrium or macro-economic structures, do not like untidiness and loose ends, and any loose ends get speedily swept up in stochastic residual terms, or ignored' (Fisher 1983: 23).

In more recent years, this blind spot on the part of some economists has been steadily corrected. For one thing, with the economics of general equilibrium fully established by the 1970s, economists began asking questions about realities that did not fit easily into the equilibrium model.

Despite this acknowledgment by economists of the entrepreneur's critical role in wealth-creation, modern Catholic social thought has generally been slow to recognise this point, let alone consider in detail the complex issue of how wealth is created. As Archbishop George Pell points out, 'it must be conceded that in the past and until Paul VI's encyclical *Populorum Progressio* and John Paul II's *Centesimus Annus*. . . . the Church had been excessively concerned with the distribution of wealth and paid insufficient attention to its production' (Pell 1992: 16). As recently as 1981, Pope John Paul II's first social encyclical, *Laborem Exercens*, focused upon the traditional categories of 'labour' and 'capital' without giving entrepreneurship *per se* any particular attention. If, however, the Church's social teaching is to be taken seriously by a whole range of potential audiences, it must be cognisant of both economic theories and economic realities. Unquestionably, issues surrounding entrepreneurship are crucial to both.

Fortunately, in more recent years, Catholic social teaching, as articulated by the Papal magisterium, has not only recognised the centrality of entrepreneurship, but also explored its moral dimension. Our purpose here is to illustrate, through analysis of various papal and conciliar texts, how these developments occurred. Consideration is then given to their possible implications for other aspects of Catholic social teaching.

A Matter of Definition

But before proceeding any further, some clarification is required of what precisely is meant by the phrase 'entrepreneurial activity'. Here religious thinkers are bound to turn to the secular intellectual disciplines for guidance, not least because it is in these realms that most thought about entrepreneurship has occurred.

There is, of course, nothing new about Christianity turning to secular thought for guidance on a range of matters. For 2000 years,

Christianity has demonstrated a remarkable capacity to learn from other streams of thought. It has done so because, as the Second Vatican Council states, the Church wishes to profit 'from the experience of past ages, from the progress of the sciences, and from the riches hidden in various cultures, through which greater light is thrown on the nature of man and new avenues to truth are opened up' (GS 44). On one level, these words constitute acknowledgment that the Church has no monopoly on discerning the truth, a position traceable to as early a Christian text as St. Paul's Letter to the Romans (1:18-2:24). Nevertheless, they also affirm that the Church can develop its knowledge of the truth – and, from a Christian viewpoint, all truth is God's truth – by engaging with others' ideas as they emerge throughout history. The advantage of such dialogue is, as Paul VI wrote, that it 'forces [the Church] to go more deeply into the subject of our investigations and to find better ways of expressing ourselves. It will be a slow process of thought, but it will result in the discovery of elements of truth in the opinion of others' (ES 83).

Naturally, there are risks involved in such an exercise. Whether out of naïvety, poor judgment, or an anxiousness never to question the ever-shifting sands of intellectual fashion, some Christians have proved all too willing to accept uncritically the propositions of those with whom they are in dialogue. This was the mistake made by some Catholic theologians who became rather indiscriminately enamoured of various strands of Marxist philosophy in the 1960s and 1970s. They would have been wise to pay heed to the Council's words in *Gaudium et Spes* which indicate that listening to others does not necessarily mean agreeing with them. Consciousness of, and attention to, the Truth of God's Revelation plays a central role in the process of discernment which occurs:

> it is the task of the whole people of God. . . . to listen to and distinguish the many voices of our time, *and to interpret them in the light of the divine Word* in order that the revealed truth may be more deeply penetrated, better understood, and more suitably presented (GS 44) [italics added].

A type of 'dialectic', then, characterises the Catholic position, this time between discoveries that emerge 'outside' the Church and the Revelation preached by the Church. The former, it is clear, are to be deciphered in light of the latter.

There have been, of course, many modern secular schools of economic thought that have given much attention to the role of the entrepreneur. The modern theory of finance has, for example, evolved from within the neo-classical tradition precisely because of many economists' efforts to study more closely how and why individuals (appropriately called 'capitalists') choose to risk investing their capital in new or existing ventures. Few, however, would dispute that the Austrian school associated with figures such as Ludwig von Mises, Friedrich von Hayek and Israel Kirzner has given sustained, systematic and sophisticated attention to the character of entrepreneurship. But this is only one reason that Catholic intellectuals may wish to look here for guidance in thinking about entrepreneurial activity. For one thing, some Catholic thinkers have already discovered that the Austrian school provides them with useful insights into a wide range of socio-economic issues. The theologian-philosopher, Michael Novak, has sought, for example, to incorporate the insights of Kirzner, Mises and Hayek into his reflections about capitalism (Novak 1989; Novak 1992). Likewise the Acton Institute's school of economic personalism has attempted a synthesis of Catholic personalist thinking with Austrian economics (Gronbacher 1998: 1-34). Across the Atlantic, another prominent Catholic social philosopher, Rocco Buttiglione, has posited that Mises' classic text, *Human Action* (1966), requires detailed attention from Catholic intellectuals. Not only, in Buttiglione's view, are the Austrians to be commended for their rejection of positivism; they also avoid excessively abstract econometrics and offer, he believes, a theory of economic value that may be reconciled with a Christian ethic.

But what is crucially important about the Austrian school, from a Catholic perspective, is that it bases its understanding of entrepreneurship upon what it calls 'praxeology': the science of human action. Human acts, according to the Austrians, are the basis of economic activity; hence, they believe that it is vital to think very carefully about the nature of the human act if one wants to arrive at reasoned conclusions about economic life. Catholic thinkers, of course, have long viewed study of the human act as a basic reference point for any serious inquiry into moral and ethical issues. It was not for trivial reasons that St. Thomas Aquinas' *Summa Theologiae*, for example, dwelt at length upon the nature of human action (ST., I-II, q.6-21).

In more recent times, Central European scholars such as the Lublin school of Thomists have revived this Catholic focus upon human action. This occurred partly under the inspiration of re-visiting Aquinas but also as a result of the Lublinists' willingness to engage in a critical dialogue with existentialism and phenomenology (Woźnicki 1986) – each of which places human action at the centre of its investigations. This resulted in the publication of works such as Karol Wojtyła's *The Acting Person* (1969). This book, like Mises' *Human Action*, took as its starting point a consideration of the human act. For this reason, Buttiglione suggests that 'a comparative reading of L. von Mises' *Human Action* with *The Acting Person* would be very engaging' (Buttiglione 1997: 379). The primary parallel between the two works is what Buttiglione calls a certain methodological individualism. Thinkers like Mises and Kirzner reduce economic phenomena 'to the agent who is engaged in it. . . the man who chooses and decides through his own action the reality around him' (Buttiglione 1997: 379). The same approach is adopted by *The Acting Person* insofar as its author is determined to break away from the modern Rousseauian propensity to view processes and structures as forces that operate almost independently of human agency. Hence, Wojtyła systematically takes his reader 'back to' human intentionality and human acts as the fundamental means through which to understand social realities.

Of course, a comparative study of *The Acting Person* and Mises' *Human Action* would be only of peripheral interest if the former was the work of a relatively unknown Central European philosopher. This, however, is not the case for the simple reason that Karol Wojtyła is better known to most people as Pope John Paul II. The wider significance, then, of *The Acting Person* and other 'Wojtyłan' pre-pontifical writings lies in the fact that distinctly Wojtyłan themes about human action have exerted a perceptible influence upon the Pope's teachings. Indeed, we will refer to some of Wojtyła's writings precisely because they help explain aspects of John Paul II's pronouncements concerning entrepreneurship

The Catholic Contribution

The bulk of Pope John Paul's teachings about personal economic initiative are to be found in that compendium of texts collectively known as 'Catholic social teaching'. It is here that scholars naturally look if they are interested in discovering specifically Catholic-Christian contributions to thinking about topics like entrepreneurship. As one Protestant theologian notes:

> Protestantism has no equivalent for the papal encyclicals of the Roman Catholic Church. . . . Its self-understanding and ecclesiology do not permit it to impose a particular point of view on its constituencies. On the other hand, Roman Catholicism, with its papal encyclicals, offers a binding, authoritative body of social teaching that is unique in the religious world (Armstrong 1993: 933).

Here one should remember that Catholic social doctrine is derived not only from reflection upon Scripture, but also Tradition, the natural law, and the Church Fathers. It also draws upon contributions of the human sciences and philosophy to thinking about social, economic and political issues (LC 72; SRS 3; CA 3, 5, 59; Charles 1998 vol. 1: 5-6). Catholic social teaching is consequently steeped in both Christian doctrine as well as the knowledge accumulated over the centuries by Christians and non-Christians alike. To this extent, it is a potentially rich source for contemplation.

Our approach, then, is to outline briefly the salient points of Austrian thought about entrepreneurship. With this framework in place, we then consider recent Catholic social teaching about entrepreneurial activity. On one level, this demonstrates that John Paul II's *Sollicitudo Rei Socialis* (1987) and *Centesimus Annus* (1991) have played a crucial role in helping the Church to recognise entrepreneurship's centrality in contemporary economic life more fully. We also see, however, that this represents development of ideas about the nature and ends of human action outlined in the Council's *Gaudium et Spes* and Pope John Paul's *Laborem Exercens*.

II. Human Action and Entrepreneurship: Insights of the Austrian School

The Austrian school is not the only group of post-Enlightenment economists to reflect upon the nature of entrepreneurship. Much discussion, for example, has occurred within the context of entrepreneurial profit theory and associated questions of distributive justice. Here the writings of J.B. Clark, Frank Knight and Joseph Schumpeter figure prominently (Clark 1899; Knight 1921; Schumpeter 1950). Then there is the neo-classical view of the entrepreneur, exemplified by Theodore Schultz, which understands entrepreneurship as performing the function of reallocating resources under conditions of disequilibrium, thereby restoring equilibrium (Schultz 1975). Hence, one should note that the Austrian model is not being focussed upon here because it is regarded as having the 'final word' on entrepreneurship. Nor should the attention that it is given in this paper be regarded as an implicit criticism of other economic schools' ideas about entrepreneurship.

The distinctiveness of the Austrian approach lies in its insistence upon grounding any reflection about entrepreneurship not in a theory of equilibrium, but rather in a science of human action. This is partly explained by the Austrian school's origins. Its 'founder', Carl Menger (1840-1921), an economist who lectured at the University of Vienna during the latter half of the nineteenth century, took methodological issues very seriously. He insisted that the way to understand large-scale phenomena was to break them down into their component parts (Hicks and Weber 1973). In 1871, Menger published *Grundsätze der Volkwirtschaftlehre* [*Principles of Economics*], a work which placed the individual at the centre of his inquiry – not, one should note, the hedonistic social atom of Benthamite utilitarianism, but rather the individual with all his diverse attachments, wishes and sentiments.

Eugen von Böhm-Bawerk (1851-1914) and Friedrich von Wieser (1851-1926) were also significant early Austrian figures. Wieser felt that to understand economic life, 'we must now, by decreasing abstraction, familiarise ourselves with typical conditions of reality' (Wieser 1927: 207). This approach influenced the outlook of Ludwig von Mises (1880-1973) who, along with Friedrich von Hayek (1899-

1992), came to prominence in the 1930s by articulating a dogged critique of centrally-planned economies and underlining the counter-productive effects of state-intervention. Among other factors, Austria's inter-war political uncertainties, which eventually culminated in the *Anschluss*, resulted in figures such as Mises emigrating, eventually, to the United States. Here he supervised the research of 'new Austrians' such as Israel Kirzner who eventually expanded the scope and parameters of Austrian economic thought, especially in regard to entrepreneurship (Vaughn 1994).

Man as Actor

Consistent with both Menger's methodological individualism and Wieser's impatience with abstraction, Austrian economic theory[2] involves working out the logical implications of the reality that man acts: the primordial fact that individuals engage in conscious actions towards chosen goals. It seeks to explain economic life by logical deduction from this *a priori* truth about man.

What, then, are the implications of this axiom of human action? For one thing, action implies that each individual's behaviour is purposive. Their acts are directed towards goals. The very fact of each human act implies that the individual has chosen certain means to reach his goals. As Mises states, 'acting man chooses, determines, and tries to reach an end' (Mises 1966: 12). Significantly, Mises also believes that it is impossible to separate action from reason, that is, 'the forethought directed towards projected acts and the afterthought that reflects upon acts done' (Mises 1933/1981: 13).[3] Hence, in Mises' view, '[a]ction and reason are congeneric and homogeneous; they may even be called two different aspects of the same thing' (Mises 1966: 39).

By approaching man from the standpoint of action, one observes that Mises is inexorably led to delineate the role played by *reason* and the *will* in each human act. In this sense, Mises' attention to human action leads him into the realm of 'philosophical anthropology': that is, philosophical reasoning based upon a view

---

[2] There are, of course, many differences in emphasis and substance in the thinking of various Austrians. Given, however, that our intention is to provide only a short and simplified introduction to their thought, we need not dwell upon these in detail.

of what man is by nature. What Mises does not assume is that an individual's choice of values or goals is wise or proper or that he has chosen the best means of attaining them. Mises simply asserts that acting man chooses goals and believes, however correctly or erroneously, that he can realise them by employing certain means.

Given that action is about the attainment of chosen ends, Mises regards action as 'always directed towards the future; it is essentially and necessarily always a planning and acting for a better future' (Mises 1966: 100). The key to the human act's role in affecting change is what Mises denotes as each individual's unique 'ability to discover causal relations that determine change and becoming in the universe'. Indeed, without this capacity to discover new causality between means and ends, there would be, as Mises notes, 'no field for human reasoning and action' (Mises 1966: 22).

By positing that it is freely chosen human acts that change the existing state of affairs, Mises indicates that the future is not 'fixed', as Marx and other determinists would have us believe. Mises points out that only a mind of perfect foresight would be able to discern precisely how the future unfolds (Mises 1966: 105). Acting humans, however, have only an imperfect knowledge. They cannot possibly know everything. This introduces an inescapable element of uncertainty into the process of thought and choice that precedes and accompanies every human act. Thus, in defining what he calls the 'categorical structure' of human action, Mises suggests that '[t]he act of choosing is always a decision among various opportunities open to the choosing individual' (Mises 1966: 45). To this extent, action is 'always speculation' (Mises 1966: 252).

But what, one may ask, motivates man to act? The most basic cause is, according to Mises, that essential uneasiness that lies within every individual, that lack of contentment that causes people to want to change themselves, others, or the world (Mises 1966: 12). From this proceeds another motive for action: that human eagerness to 'substitute a more satisfactory state of affairs for a less satisfactory one' (Mises 1966: 13). This eagerness must, however, be complemented by the expectation that action will indeed bring about

---

[3] What Mises' view of reason and action cannot, however, account for, is that the fact that people *can* act without reason, as in the instance of the acts of an insane person.

the envisaged better state of affairs (Mises 1966: 14). Hence, one may say that action will not occur unless there is a clear *incentive* to act as well as a strong possibility that the act will indeed bring about a more satisfactory state of affairs for its enactor.

Acting Man as Entrepreneur

It is upon this paradigm of the causes, character, scope and context of human action that the Austrians build their understanding of entrepreneurship. Given that every freely-willed act is necessarily a speculation upon the uncertain conditions of the future, one may posit, as Mises does, that every acting human is an entrepreneur (Mises 1966: 252). From this viewpoint, an individual's 'function' as manager, worker or owner is irrelevant. *Everyone* acts in light of their imperfect knowledge of the future.

Nonetheless, economics also uses the word 'entrepreneur' to describe those who are, as Mises puts it, 'especially eager to profit from adjusting production to the expected changes in conditions, those who have more initiative, more venturesomeness, and a quicker eye than the crowd, the pushing and promoting pioneers of economic improvement' (Mises 1966: 255). People, in short, do not act in the same way or with the same speed and dexterity in response to changes in information furnished by the market. This, one may say, reflects the truth that natural inequality – in the sense that not all people are gifted in the same way – reigns in this area as well.

Kirzner points out that entrepreneurial responses to such changes in information should not be understood as a process of calculation. Rather, the entrepreneurial dimension concerns that element of a decision that involves 'a shrewd and wise assessment of the realities (both present and future) within the context of which the decision must be made' (Kirzner 1985: 17). 'Assessment' is the key word here. It highlights the reality that each person's knowledge is limited and that each individual's acts consequently take place in, and contribute to, a context of uncertainty. For if there was no uncertainty, decision-making would merely call for the precise calculation of facts and options, in which case humans would be nothing more than robots. The reality is, however, that no matter how accurate one's calculations, a decision will be poor if its entrepreneurial-speculative component involves poor judgement.

Uncertainty, of course, means that people make errors, both of judgement and omission. There are possibilities that they do not perceive. This, as Kirzner stresses, suggests that '[s]cope for entrepreneurship. . . . appears to be grounded in the possibility of discovering error' (Kirzner 1985: 51). One may go further and point out that if man lived in circumstances in which there was no error, there would be no scope for discovery and speculation in human action.

The question consequently arises of how entrepreneurial discovery comes about. In what amounts to a clear elaboration upon Mises' thought, Kirzner argues that '[m]an acts, in light of the future as he envisages it, to enhance his position in that future' (Kirzner 1985: 54). Put another way, people look through 'the fog' of the future that looms before them, seeking opportunities to actualise hitherto unknown potentialities. The term used by Kirzner to describe this process of searching is 'alertness'. Without this element, people would not be able to act freely at all: their blindness to the future would rob them of any framework for freely willed and reasoned action. Alertness, then, 'embraces the awareness of the ways the human agent can, by imaginative, bold leaps of faith and determination, in fact *create* the future for which his present acts are designed' (Kirzner 1985: 56).

Given the importance of alertness to entrepreneurial discovery, one is bound to ask what 'turns it on'? What is it that causes and encourages people to seek out opportunities to create their future? Mises, we recall, states that people will not act unless they have an incentive to do so. Building upon this observation, Kirzner adds that people tend to notice that which it is in their interest to notice (Kirzner 1985: 28). Hence, if entrepreneurial alertness is to be 'switched on', it would seem that the possible opportunities must offer some direct gain to the potential discoverer himself. Indeed, the incentive has to be particularly strong if it is to reveal potentialities that up to the present have hitherto remained undiscovered by anyone else.

To summarise, then, the character of entrepreneurship as understood by the Austrians.

• There is a critical link between the 'open-ended' character of human acts and entrepreneurship, due to the inherently speculative dimension of human action. Room for entrepreneurial acts exists because of perpetual uncertainty about how the future will unfold. This uncertainty proceeds from the limits to man's capacity to grasp the entirety of the changing conditions of economic life that are constantly unfolding before him.

• The entrepreneurial-act involves establishing equivalence between the individual's self-envisaged future and the future as it will in fact unfold. It means discovering error by being alert to unrealised opportunities that loom through the fog of the future. Such alertness allows people to actualise hidden potentialities and effectively create their own future and shape that of others. In all these senses, entrepreneurial activity is, in essence, a highly intellectual exercise because its basic dynamics occur within the human mind.

• The key to maintaining alertness is the existence of substantive incentives for potential entrepreneurs.

Convergences – Divergences

From the standpoint of economics, there are, of course, many criticisms that may be made of the Austrian understanding of entrepreneurship. It seems, for example, to draw, at least implicitly, too sharp a distinction between the initiators of risky ventures and the providers of capital, seeing entrepreneurship as primarily characteristic of the former. Surely the latter are almost equally crucial to wealth-creation, insofar as they too must be convinced of, or 'see', the potential to be actualised and be willing to take as many, or even more, risks as the person with the new idea. Otherwise, they would hardly commit the necessary capital and/ or financial acumen required for the success of any venture, the absence of which necessarily results in an entrepreneurial insight remaining fallow.

There is, nonetheless, much in the Austrian paradigm of entrepreneurship that can be affirmed by Christians. By referring, for example, to man as a creature perpetually gripped by a certain unease and discontent, Mises not only echoes Locke and Leibniz, but also St. Augustine who wrote: 'You have made us for yourself, and our hearts find no peace until they rest in you' (Con., I, 1).

Like Mises, Augustine recognised that there is an insatiability within human beings, which Christianity has always regarded as proceeding from the human spirit's endless striving for the transcendent.

Similarly, Catholic thinkers should find much to commend in the Austrians' decision to take as their starting point the undeniable fact that man acts, and that free will and reason are the primary shapers of human acts. The Catholic study of ethics proceeds from a similar basis insofar as it involves the study of voluntary human conduct including 'all actions, and also omissions, over which man exercises personal control, because he understands and wills these actions (and omissions) in relation to some end that he has in view' (Brown 1967: 152). Aquinas himself observes that to deny that people are each masters of their own acts is to claim something 'impossible, and destructive of all moral philosophy and social-political life [*politicae conversationis*]' (ScG, II, chp.60, n.5). A contemporary neo-Thomist, John Finnis, points out that the whole tenor of Aquinas' work leads to the conclusion that

> human actions, and the societies constituted by human action, cannot be adequately understood as if they were merely (1) natural occurrences, (2) contents of thoughts, or (3) products of techniques of mastering natural materials. . . . True, there are elements in human life and behaviour . . . such as the workings of one's digestion, or one's instinct and emotions, which can and should be understood as objects (subject-matter) of natural science. . . . But human actions and societies cannot be adequately described, explained, justified, or criticised unless they are understood as also, and centrally, the carrying out of free choices (Finnis 1998: 22).

Moreover, the understanding of human reason that underlies the Austrian paradigm echoes important themes in Christianity. While insisting that man can attain knowledge of higher truths, the Church has always warned against the hubristic notion that any one individual is capable of knowing everything – if they did, then they would be, as the serpent points out in Genesis, 'like gods' (Gen 3:4-6). If anything, Mises and Kirzner are even more insistent on the limits to human knowledge. Their paradigm of entrepreneurship posits that people are constantly discovering errors that have previously escaped others' attention. There is something very human about their portrait of entrepreneurial-acting-man constantly searching in a rather fumbling fashion through the fog of the future for unknown possibilities to discover.

Given their vision of entrepreneurship, it is little wonder that the Austrians are rather sceptical of those forms of economics that rely heavily upon mathematical modelling and which consequently encounter difficulties in reflecting the dynamism and unpredictability proceeding from entrepreneurial activity. In this regard, Catholic social thinkers should be rather sympathetic to Austrian praxeology precisely because it 'rescues' economics from the mathematical formalism that neo-classical theory adopted from Newtonian mechanical physics. As noted by the economist and Anglican social thinker, Lord Griffiths, the Enlightenment encouraged people to think of economics as a system and to view God as a type of 'grand mathematician' who created the world as a complex machine that runs according to its own established mathematical principles (Griffiths 1984: 107-108). In certain respects, this perspective is difficult to reconcile with the Catholic view of society as the interaction of persons and communities with free will, not to mention the Christian vision of God as a loving Father who became incarnate (*et homo factus est*) in the person of Jesus Christ.

We cannot, however, avoid noting that there are aspects of the Austrian understanding of entrepreneurial activity that are difficult to reconcile with Catholic teaching. One concerns the essentially utilitarian premises that inform Mises' view of what constitutes the more satisfactory state of affairs that acting man attempts to realise. Mises believes that '[t]here is no standard of greater or lesser satisfaction other than individual judgements of value' (Mises 1966: 14).[4] Catholicism expresses a quite different position. It has always held that there is an *objective* hierarchy of values that all people are able to discern, thanks to God's Revelation as well through use of their reason. At the summit of this hierarchy are moral-spiritual goods such as truth, beauty and friendship. Attaining these goods provides man with the greatest happiness in this life precisely because they bring him closest to God. Hence, while the use and possession of material goods is essential for a person's physical and moral growth, they should not be mistaken as the highest goods attainable by human beings (GS 35; PP 19-21; SRS 28-29; CA 36).

But to be fair to Mises, one should note that his praxeology does 'not pretend to know anything about the intentions of an absolute and objective mind' or 'about the plans which God or Nature or *Weltgeist* or manifest Destiny is trying to realise in directing the universe and human affairs' (Mises 1966: 28-29). Nor does Mises believe that people are entitled to act in ways that are completely oblivious to the interest of others. The concept of reciprocity figures in his thought:

> Morality consists in the regard for the necessary requirements of social existence that must be demanded of each individual. . . . as a member of society, a man must take into consideration, in everything he does, not only his immediate advantage, but also the necessity of affirming society as such. For the life of the individual in society is possible only by virtue of social cooperation (Mises 1985: 33).

Here Mises comes close to affirming that people must act in ways that reflect their consciousness of the existence of what the Second Vatican Council called 'the common good', defined as 'the sum total of social conditions which allow people, either as groups or as individuals, to reach their fulfilment more fully and more easily' (GS 26). Certainly, the idea of the common good was not extraneous to Mises' thought. In another of his works, Mises even concluded that 'the policy of liberalism is the policy of the common good, the policy of subjecting particular interests to the public welfare' (Mises 1981: 456).

There is, however, a missing dimension to the Austrian paradigm of entrepreneurial acts. Broadly speaking, Catholic intellectuals would agree with Mises that human acts 'create' the future, that they are forever shaping the world. But is this the limit of the effects

---

[4] Not all Austrians, one should note, were or are utilitarian in their philosophical presumptions. Hayek, for example, believed that Mises' rationalist-utilitarian outlook was at the heart of what Hayek believed to be certain problems with Mises' critique of socialism (Hayek 1994: 72-73).

of human action? Following in the footsteps of Aristotle and the thinkers of Antiquity, Catholicism has always insisted that each freely willed human act shapes not only the world but also the act's author. Throughout the centuries, Catholic theologians have regarded this dimension of human action as more important than the same act's external effect. By bringing this insight to bear upon the Church's attitude towards entrepreneurship, Catholic social teaching has demonstrated that it is capable not only of complementing secular thinking about entrepreneurial acts, but of endowing entrepreneurship with a moral and theological grandeur of its own.

III. Catholicism, Human Acts and Entrepreneurship

The Scholastic Tradition

Strictly speaking, Nell-Breuning was incorrect to suggest that Catholic thinking had largely ignored the entrepreneur. He was, however, not alone in making this error. Hayek, for example, contended that Catholicism's embrace of Aristotelian ethics resulted in the Medieval and early Modern Church developing an 'anti-commercial attitude' as well as its condemnation of the charging of interest as usury (Hayek 1988: 47).

In the case of the latter claim, one need only note that medieval theologians actually played a major role in *changing* the Church's negative view of interest-charging (Finnis 1998: 200-210; Noonan 1957; Roover 1967). As Franz-Xaver Kaufmann notes: 'In Europe, the Church debated the distinction between usury and interest, and from the twelfth century onwards, the scholastic literature accepted and codified them. This recognition contributed to the growing sophistication of economic discourse; for instance, concepts such as risk and opportunity came to be invoked with increasing frequency (Kaufmann 1997). Nor is it accurate to view medieval and early modern Catholicism as having an 'anti-commercial' mindset. Certainly, there were some medieval theologians such as the fourteenth century Viennese nominalist, Henry of Langenstein, who were implacably opposed to the free market. Others, such as the twelfth century scholastic, Peter of Lombard, went so far as to denounce trade itself as a sinful occupation (Roover 1963: 76-81).

Such figures were, however, rather marginal. Lombard's thesis, for example, was directly refuted by Hugh of St. Victor (1096-1141) who underlined the tremendous benefits of commerce:

> The pursuit of commerce reconciles nations, calms wars, strengthens peace, and commutes the private good of individuals into the common benefit of all. . . . Commerce penetrates the secret places of the world, approaches shores unseen, explores fearful wildernesses, and in tongues unknown and with barbaric peoples carries on the trade of mankind (cited in Fanfani 1933: 152).

Similar thoughts are to be found in the writings of Albertus Magnus and his great pupil, Aquinas, as well as St. Bonaventure and Pope Innocent V. Each of these scholars set forth a quite benevolent view of trade. All regarded, for example, merchant activity, exchange and the division of labour as essential for satisfying the population's needs (Roover 1963: 82-87). Aristotle, by contrast, believed that those who engaged in commerce seek not so much the well-being of a household, but rather the endless increase of their own wealth; he consequently viewed commercial activity for profit as essentially unnecessary and somewhat disreputable (Pol. I.3). Rejecting this position, Aquinas argued that people *could* involve themselves in commerce for many good reasons that were of benefit to society: these included the conservation and storage of goods; the importation of goods useful to the polity; and the transportation of goods from places where they are abundant to places where they are scarce (ST., II-II, q.77, a.4). A reasonable profit for such activities was, in Aquinas' view, quite legitimate inasmuch as it represented payment of services rendered by work [*quasi stipendium laboris*].

Following the founding of the Jesuit order in 1540, scholastic thinkers such as Luis de Molina, S.J., (1535-1624) and Francisco Suárez, S.J., (1548-1617) assumed a prominent role in advocating, as Henry Robertson establishes, 'enterprise, freedom of speculation and the expansion of trade as a social benefit' (Robertson 1973: 164). Similar propositions were advanced by Dominicans such as Francisco de Vitoria (1480-1546) and Domingo de Soto (1495-1560) as well as other Spanish late scholastics associated with the University of Salamanca such as Luis Saravía de la Calle. The latter's study of the complex issue of the 'just price', for instance, resulted in the conclusion that the just price was the market price determined by supply and demand (presuming the absence of fraud, force, and monopoly) which in turn resulted from the common estimation of consumers in the market (Saravía de la Calle 1544/1949: 109-118). Taking a broader view, Soto described the emergence of markets and commerce as evidence of civilisational development:

> Mankind progresses from imperfection to perfection. For this reason, in the beginning barter was sufficient as man was rude and ignorant and had few necessities. But afterward, with the development of a more educated, civilised and distinguished life, the need to create new forms of trade arose. Among them the most respectable is commerce (DII., VI, q.II, a.2).

This statement prefigures similar propositions about commerce advanced by Scottish Enlightenment figures such as Adam Ferguson in his *Essay on the History of Civil Society* (1767/1966: 181-190).

Given this history of affirming commerce, the market, and trade in general, it appears that many contemporary Catholic critics of business and markets would do well to acquire a deeper understanding of their own tradition. Even entrepreneurship did not escape the scrutiny of scholastic theologians. One of the most important figures in this regard was St. Bernardino of Siena (1380-1444). Although Bernardino specified that the occupations of trade and entrepreneurship could lead to sin, he pointed out that this was true of every other occupation – including that of bishop, priest, and theologian.

While not viewing entrepreneurs as *ipso facto* moral heroes, Bernardino describes at length the rare qualities and virtues that are commonly exhibited by private entrepreneurs and businessmen. One is efficiency [*industria*], which includes knowledge of prices, qualities and costs, the ability to assess risks [*pericula*] and estimate profit opportunities. 'Very few', Bernardino declares, 'are capable of doing this'. Entrepreneurs must be responsible and attentive to detail, and trouble and toil are also integral to private business endeavours. The rational and orderly conduct of business is another virtue highlighted by Bernardino, as is integrity and the prompt settlement of accounts (Bernardino 1591/1928; cf. Roover 1963). Given the difficulty of combining these qualities and virtues, Bernardino argues that the entrepreneur properly earns the profits that keep him in business and compensate him for his hardships. They represent, according to Bernardino, a legitimate return to the entrepreneur for his labour, expenses, and risks undertaken.

But why do such qualities count as 'virtues'? Bernardino does not spell this out, presumably because he would have assumed that his medieval audience would have generally understood what is meant by this phrase. Unfortunately, as Alasdair MacIntyre points out in his seminal work, *After Virtue*, any common understanding or even basic knowledge of the meaning of this term has largely disappeared within contemporary Western societies (MacIntyre 1981). By 'virtue', Bernardino almost certainly had in mind one of its classic Aristotelian-Thomistic meanings: a moral habit of action that reflects man's consistent free choice of moral good (ST., I-II, q.40, a.1, c; I-II, q.34, a.2, ad.1). Hence in Bernardino's schema, it is the entrepreneur's *consistent acts* of industriousness, efficiency, risk-assessment, and integrity that allow him to actualise these human potentialities as moral virtues. As Aristotle remarks in his *Ethics*, 'Moral virtues, like crafts [*technē*], are acquired by practice and habituation' (NE II.1).

From this perspective, it soon becomes apparent that there are actually two dimensions to human action: its 'outer' effect upon the world and its 'inner' effect within its author. In his *Quaestiones Disputatae de Veritate* (q.8, a.6c), Aquinas explained this in the following manner:

> Action is of two sorts: one sort — action [*actio*] in a strict sense — issues from the agent into something external to change it. . . . the other sort — properly called activity [*operatio*] — does not issue into something external but remains within the agent itself perfecting it.

One should not be too surprised that neither Mises nor Kirzner discuss action's inner moral effects. They are, after all, writing within the discipline of economics rather than that of moral philosophy or theology. It is, nonetheless, by focussing upon this understanding of human action that Catholic social teaching has been able to revive the Church's appreciation of entrepreneurship in the closing decades of the twentieth century, a recovery that has its immediate roots in the social teaching of the Second Vatican Council.

Human Activity and Creation

Despite the flowering of Catholic thought about economics that occurred between the eleventh and seventeenth centuries, the Church's interest in such matters was beginning to wane by the beginning of the eighteenth century. For one thing, the tremendous intellectual and missionary forces unleashed by the Counter-Reformation began to dissipate (Hsia 1998: 194-209). Much energy was also absorbed by internal theological disputes, such as the debates over Jansenism and Febronianism (Daniel-Rops 1964: 227-300). Moreover, the Church was distracted by the emergence of new problems, such as the many continental European *philosophes* who viewed Catholicism rather negatively. It was, after all, Voltaire who coined the phrase *'Ecrasez l'infâme!'* – destroy the infamous one, by which he meant the Catholic Church. Accompanying this intellectual hostility was the determination of the absolutist Catholic monarchies of Portugal, Spain, France and the Habsburg hereditary lands to undermine the Church's institutional autonomy within their territories. Their policies culminated in Pope Clement XIV's reluctant suppression of the Jesuit order in 1773 by the papal bull, *Dominus ac redemptor*. The upheavals of 1789, of course, resulted in Catholicism's chief intellectual institutions being destroyed by the fury of the French Revolution which, after 1791, embraced a specifically anti-Catholic dimension (Johnson 1976: 357-363).

Nor did the post-revolutionary period change matters dramatically. On the Continent, the Church tended to ally itself with the interests of monarchy and generally opposed separation of church and state. This did nothing to endear it to large numbers of Continental liberals, many of whom adopted an ultra-rationalist and often militantly atheistic outlook on human affairs. As Hayek lamented at the first Mont Pèlerin meeting in 1947, it was this 'aggressive rationalism which would recognise no values except those whose utility (for an ultimate purpose never disclosed) could be demonstrated by individual reason and which presumed that science was competent to tell us not only what is but what ought to be' that alienated large numbers of Christians from the cause of free societies to which they would otherwise have been quite sympathetic (Hayek 1947/1992: 244).[5] By 1891, however, the full social and economic changes unleashed by the Industrial Revolution, the growing spectre of Marxism, and the increasing interest of European Catholic intellectuals in social and economic questions (Misner 1991), caused the Papacy, on the initiative of Leo XIII, to renew decisively the Church's interest in such issues.

Looking through the resultant early encyclicals of modern Catholic social teaching, one finds very few positive statements about business or entrepreneurs in general. Instead, they seem to have been blamed for much of the social unrest that characterised many European nations at the time. In *Rerum Novarum*, for example, Leo XIII attacked socialism and vigorously defended private property (RN 4-10, 14-15, 17). Nonetheless, Pope Leo had hard words for that 'small number of rich men [who] have been able to lay upon the teeming masses of the labouring poor a yoke little better than that of slavery itself' (RN 3).

Such censures of business are absent from the main body of social teaching produced by the Second Vatican Council, its Pastoral Constitution *Gaudium et Spes* (1965). This document also differs from previous Catholic social teaching by giving very explicit attention to the nature of human action. Throughout the first half of the twentieth century, much was written about the meaning of human action by existentialists, phenomenologists, Marxists, as well

---

[5]   In *The Constitution of Liberty*, Hayek reiterates his abhorrence of nineteenth century Continental liberalism's ultra-rationalist and anti-religious tendencies, and argues that 'true liberalism has no quarrel with religion' (Hayek 1960: 407). The same point is made in earlier Hayek writings. In 1944, for example, he contended that 'if a more liberal outlook is to be fostered among the great masses. . . . any such effort must carefully avoid that hostile attitude towards religion characteristic of much of Continental liberalism, which has done a great deal to drive hosts of decent people into opposition to any kind of liberalism' (Hayek 1944/1992: 210). Elsewhere Hayek stated that the European continent would have been spared much misery if the liberalism associated with Lord Acton 'had prevailed instead of the intellectualist version of liberalism which by its fierce and intolerant attitude towards religion divided Europe hopelessly into two camps' (Hayek 1953: 461).

as liberals such as Mises. It is not surprising, then, that *Gaudium et Spes* spends much time explaining the Church's view of human activity. In doing so, it outlined a paradigm of human action that would be drawn upon by John Paul II to re-think the nature of entrepreneurship.

One of *Gaudium et Spes*' dominant motifs is that the pace of change in modern society is increasing. The Council states quite explicitly that 'History itself is accelerating [*acceleratur*] on so rapid a course that individuals can scarcely keep pace with it. . . . And so the human race is passing from a relatively static conception of the nature of things to a more dynamic and evolutionary conception' (GS 5). In short, rapid change is understood as a new constant.[6] Moreover, the Council traces this dynamism to the essentially *creative* nature of human activity, especially that of human work:

> Throughout the course of the centuries, men have laboured to better the circumstances of their lives through a monumental amount of individual and collective effort. To believers, this point is settled: considered in itself, such human activity accords with God's will. For man, created to God's image, received a mandate to subject to himself the earth and all that it contains, and to govern the world with justice and holiness [refers to Genesis 1:26-27]; a mandate to relate himself and the totality of things to Him who was to be acknowledged as the Lord and Creator of all. Thus, through the dominion of all things by man, the name of God would be made wonderful through all the earth (GS 34).

The reference to Genesis in this extract is important. On one level, it provides the text above with its understanding of man as the *imago Dei* given dominion over the world. Made in the Creator's image, people are charged with the responsibility of unfolding the Creator's work. Human acts of work are therefore understood by

---

[6] This, however, is balanced by the Council's stress that in the midst of this seemingly perpetual acceleration some things remain fixed and immutable: 'the Church affirms, too, that underlying all that changes there are many things that do not change, and that have their ultimate foundation in Christ who is the same yesterday, today, and forever' (GS 10).

the Council as *proceeding from* and *co-operative with* God's creative Act.

In another sense, however, the passage above provides us with a biblical insight into the inner dynamics of human activity itself. The word 'Creator' implies a free person. This suggests that the Act of creation was a free act, an act that did not flow from necessity. Moreover, it was an act of intelligence. God knew what He was doing and He willed it. On this basis, it is possible to draw the following conclusions. One is that nothing is inevitable. In carrying out their mandate to subdue the earth, people need to be *attentive* to the possibilities for change. Second, it is the fact that human acts involve the use of reason and free will that makes them creative. Creativity, in short, comes from within man; it is one of those things that distinguish human beings from the animals.

Having established this biblical and theological framework, the Council begins to focus upon man himself. *Gaudium et Spes* explains that the human act simultaneously shapes not only the world in which man lives, but also its immediate initiator:

> Just as human activity proceeds from man, so it is ordered to man. For when a man works, he not only alters things and society, he develops himself as well [*se ipsum perficit*]. He learns much, he cultivates his resources, he goes outside of himself and beyond himself [*extra se et supra se*]. Rightly understood, this kind of growth is of greater value than any external riches which can be garnered (GS 35).

Marie-Dominique Chenu, O.P., interprets this passage as indicating that in building up the world, man can simultaneously perfect himself (Chenu 1986: 21). Chenu omits to note, however, that the words above portray work's transforming effect upon man as more important than its external impact.

Precisely what the Council believes man should 'become' through acts of work is obviously more than some vague notion of 'personal development'. It involves some degree of transcendence 'beyond' himself (*extra se et supra se*). What the Council primarily has in mind is man's realisation of moral good. This is apparent from its identification of true human progress with the spreading 'on earth [of] the fruits of our nature and our enterprise – human dignity, brotherly communion, and freedom' (GS 39). By portraying these goods as the products of human nature and enterprise, the Council indicates that they are integral to man, but must be realised through his actions. This is, of course, the classic natural law position expressed in the Aristotelian-Thomistic proposition that people must actualise their potential.

Already it should be apparent that there is ample scope within the Council's paradigm of human action for developing Catholic teaching about entrepreneurship. Apart from the obvious potential of the creativity motif, *Gaudium et Spes*' picture of man freely actualising the potentialities of the world and his own nature conveys the same sense of human dynamism and continuous discovery that Mises and Kirzner associate with entrepreneurship. But instead of developing these points, the Council prefers to speak more generally – and vaguely – of the need to 'encourage technical progress and the spirit of enterprise. . . . eagerness for creativity and improvement and. . . . adoption of production methods and all serious efforts of people engaged in production' (GS 64). Significantly, there is no mention of the virtues that St. Bernardino insisted are acquired through entrepreneurial activity.

Paul VI, by contrast, does refer to this dimension of private economic initiative in his 1967 social encyclical, *Populorum Progressio*. Though often attacked for its statements concerning the efficacy of planning (Bauer 1982), this encyclical acknowledges that material and moral benefits do flow from entrepreneurial acts:

> By dint of intelligent thought and hard work, man gradually uncovers the hidden laws of nature and learns to make better use of natural resources. As he takes control over his way of life, he is stimulated to undertake new investigations and fresh discoveries, to take prudent risks and launch new ventures, to act responsibly and give of himself unselfishly (PP 25).

Prudent risk-taking and a sense of responsibility are, one recalls, two of the virtues that Bernardino believed people to be capable of developing through entrepreneurial acts. What is, however, missing from Pope Paul's words is an explanation of *how* acting in an entrepreneurial fashion allows people to acquire such moral goods.

Nor does Pope Paul elaborate on *what* drives people to be entrepreneurial. Significantly, these are two gaps in modern Catholic social teaching that John Paul II has gradually corrected in his three social encyclicals, *Laborem Exercens* (1981), *Sollicitudo Rei Socialis* (1987), and *Centesimus Annus* (1991). In this regard, Catholic social teaching owes much to Pope John Paul's pre-pontifical intellectual focus upon discerning the meaning and nature of human action.

The Wojtyłan Dimension
Before his election as John Paul II in October 1978, Cardinal Karol Wojtyła combined his pastoral duties as Archbishop of Kraków with an academic career as a moral philosopher. Apart from holding the Chair of Ethics at the Catholic University of Lublin from 1954 onwards (four years before being appointed a bishop), Wojtyła wrote five theological-philosophical books prior to 1978 as well as numerous papers which were published in religious and secular journals throughout Western and Eastern Europe.

Given that he was living in a Marxist-Leninist state, Wojtyła was not as free as he may have liked to write about certain topics, especially those which directly challenged fundamental features of Marxist-Leninist command economies such as their suppression of private entrepreneurship. It is clear, however, that after 1952, Wojtyła's philosophical interests were primarily in the nature and meaning of human action. It was not until he became Pope that Wojtyła was in a position, like Mises, to apply his conclusions about human action to economic life.

In his pre-pontifical works, Wojtyła takes the view that if man is to be good – to be virtuous – he requires greater knowledge of what he is. To unravel this mystery, Wojtyła's major philosophical text, *The Acting Person*, proceeds from the premise that 'action *reveals* the person'. But immediately one thinks about human actions, Wojtyła says, one sees that their uniqueness is derived from their moral significance: 'Morality constitutes their intrinsic feature and what may be viewed as their specific profile, which is not to be found in acting that assumes agents other than a person' (Wojtyła 1979a: 11). The acts of animals, for instance, lack a moral dimension because animals are not persons.

While Wojtyła accepts the essential accuracy of Boethius' definition of the person – '*persona est rationalis naturae individua substantia*' (Wojtyła 1979a: 73) – he also believes that 'neither the concept of the "rational nature" nor that of its individualisation seems to express fully the specific completeness expressed in the concept of the person' (Wojtyła 1979a: 73-74). In short, it does not sufficiently underline the significance of human acts for that person. For this reason, Wojtyła employs the concept of *subject* because '[i]t is in the subject as a being that every dynamic structure is rooted, every acting and happening' (Wojtyła 1979a: 72).

By drawing attention to the person's character as a subject of acts,[7] Wojtyła is able to 'rethink' man's nature in terms of being the support and author of actions which are of profound significance for him as a person. Here it is crucial to note *The Acting Person*'s distinctions between the 'transitive' and 'intransitive' dimensions of human acts:

> [action] is both transitive and intransitive with regard to the person. . . . In the inner dimension of the person, human action is at once both transitory and relatively lasting, inasmuch as its effects, which are to be viewed in relation to efficacy and self-determination, that is to say, to the person's engagement in freedom, last longer than the action itself. . . . [For] [h]uman actions once performed do not vanish without a trace: they leave their moral value, which constitutes an objective reality intrinsically cohesive with the person, and thus a reality profoundly subjective (Wojtyła 1979a: 150-151).

Put more simply, an act's 'transitive' dimension refers to its effects outside their human subject or author. The same act, however, has an 'intransitive' effect that persists within its human subject long

---

[7] 'Subject: In the logical sphere it is that concept of which something must be predicated and which itself cannot be a predicate. In its ontological sense it is correlative to accident; the support of an accident, be that support another and more basic accident, or, ultimately, the substance, is called *subject*' (Bigongiari 1981: 214). The use of subject in AP conforms to both senses of the word. Man is the 'support' of acts; at the same time, acts are 'predicated upon' man.

after the action has occurred. The word 'intransitive' indicates that every freely-willed human act proceeding from man morally shapes him as a person. Their inner effect is an inescapable objective moral reality for man; yet because the person is also the subject of his acts, these acts simultaneously constitute a 'profoundly subjective' reality.

There is little question that Wojtyła's distinction between human action's transitive and intransitive dimensions has been influenced by Aristotelian-Thomistic thought. The proof is to be found in a 1977 article where Wojtyła states:

> As I understand St. Thomas' thought, human activity is simultaneously *transitive* and *intransitive*. It is transitive insofar as it tends *beyond the subject*, seeks an expression and an effect in the external world, and is objectified in some product. It is intransitive, on the other hand, insofar as it *remains in the subject*, [and] determines the subject's immanent quality or value (Wojtyła 1977: 516).

Though Wojtyła does not specify which of Aquinas' writings he has in mind, there is at least a strong possibility that he is referring to Aquinas' distinction between *actio* and *operatio* in *Quaestiones Disputatae de Veritate*. Significantly, in defining the moral good (or evil) that the human subject acquires through his freely-willed acts, Wojtyła also employs Aristotelian-Thomist categories:

> I fulfil myself through good; evil brings me non-fulfilment . . . Self-fulfilment is actualised in the act by its moral value, that is, through good which occurs only in the act as such (*per modum actus*). The experience of morality indicates further possibilities of further grounding and consolidating in the subject both good as a moral value and evil. The ethics of Aristotle and Thomas Aquinas. . . . speak of habits which are moral abilities which may be either virtues or vices. In all this there are the manifold forms of self-fulfilment, or, on the contrary, of non-fulfilment (Wojtyła 1979b: 287).

Clearly, Wojtyła believes that if one wants to understand the nature of the moral life, then an understanding of the character of human action as well as the concept of man as the human subject of acts is fundamental. Turning now to John Paul II's social teachings, we see that he has integrated these 'Wojtyłan' emphases with the paradigm of human acts outlined in *Gaudium et Spes*, a synthesis that results in the most positive Catholic statements about entrepreneurial activity in centuries.

Man as the Creative Subject of Work

In an echo of earlier papal teaching, Pope John Paul has hard words in *Laborem Exercens* for businessmen and entrepreneurs of the late eighteenth and early nineteenth centuries (LE 19). The Pope is, however, careful to stress that he is reflecting upon the past rather than the present. Of more interest, for our purposes, is Pope John Paul's reiteration of the Council's understanding of work as a creative action. Repeating the Council's point that history seems to be undergoing 'periods of "acceleration" [*accelerantur*]' (LE 4), the Pope focuses upon the two Genesis verses in which man is described as created 'in the image of God. . . . male and female' (Gen 1:27) and told to 'Be fruitful and multiply, and fill the earth and subdue it' (Gen 1:28). These verses, John Paul states, 'indirectly indicate [work] as an activity for man to carry out in the world'. They also specify that '[m]an is the image of God partly through the mandate received from his Creator to subdue, to dominate, the earth. In carrying out this mandate, man, every human being, reflects the very action of the Creator of the universe' (LE 4).

John Paul's position is thus the same as the Council's. As Alberto Gini states: 'Although *Laborem Exercens* never uses the terms "co-creation" or "co-creator", John Paul II makes it clear that the divine action of creativity and human work are dynamically interrelated' (Gini 1992: 230). Every person is therefore a potential source of creativity.

Having affirmed the Council's vision of human work-acts, John Paul elaborates upon their effects. To express his ideas, the Pope draws upon both *Gaudium et Spes* and *The Acting Person*. *Laborem Exercens* distinguishes between work in the objective sense and work in the subjective sense. The former is first described as 'work understood as a "transitive" activity, that is to say an activity beginning in the human subject and directed towards an external object' (LE 4). Whilst these words parallel *Gaudium et Spes*' position that work shapes the outside world, the characteristically 'Wojtyłan' language used in this extract adds precision to the teaching about how this occurs. The identification of man as subject distinguishes man as the *support* and *predicate* of his work. It is on these premises that one can say, like the Council, that 'work proceeds from man'.

Paragraph 5 of *Laborem Exercens* elaborates upon the meaning of work as a 'transitive' activity. It speaks of 'the meaning of *work in an objective sense*, which finds expression in the various epochs of culture and civilisation'. To this extent, work in the transitive-objective sense expresses man's dominion over the world and the material progress that ensues from it.

Laborem Exercens then considers what may be called, to use a Wojtyłan term, work's *intransitive* dimension: work in the subjective sense.

> Man has to subdue the earth and dominate it, because as the 'image of God' he is a person, that is to say, a subjective being [*animans subiectivus*] capable of acting in a planned and rational way [*capax ad agendum ratione praestituta et rationali*], capable of deciding about himself [*capax ad deliberandum de se*] and with a tendency to self-realisation [*eoque contendens ut se ipsum perficiat*]. *As a person, man is therefore the subject of work.* As a person he works [*opus facit*], he performs various actions [*actiones*] belonging to the work process; independently of their objective content, these actions must all serve to realise his humanity, to fulfil the calling to be a person that is his by reason of his very humanity [*vocationi, ex qua est persona quaeque vi ipsius humanitatis eius et propria*] (LE 6).

Understanding the full meaning of this paragraph is crucial if one is to grasp Pope John Paul's development of Catholic teaching about entrepreneurship. It explains that man's work has an 'intransitive' effect upon him, an effect which begins with man's use of his unique capacities as a person and a subjective being; that is, *acting* (the property of a subject) as his *reason* tells him and making decisions, or what one may call exercising his *will* (properties of a person). In other words, when the person-subject acts, he not only chooses an external object; he simultaneously makes a *choice about himself.* As the encyclical notes, work's ethical value 'remains linked to the fact that the one who carries it out is a person, a conscious and free subject, that is to say a subject that decides about himself [*de se ipso deliberans*]' (LE 6).

The second point emerging from the extract above is that what we call 'work' is actually quite a complex activity. It presupposes, for example, the domination of our instincts through the use of reason and free will. This suggests that there are different dimensions to what is known as 'work'. Its intellectual dimension enables man to 'see' things, and thereby provides him with a vision of something that can be newly actualised. Thus, in the very nature of human work, it is possible to detect what Mises and Kirzner regard as a vital seed of what they call entrepreneurship.

In *Laborem Exercens,* however, the Pope does not elaborate upon this aspect of his thinking about human work. Instead, he continues to explore its ethical nature by specifying that man's self-realisation as a person through human work-acts involves the acquisition of moral good. Though work involves toil, John Paul states that

> in spite of all this toil – perhaps, in a sense, because of it – work is a good thing for man. Even though it bears the mark of a *bonum arduum* in the terminology of St. Thomas [refers to ST., I-II, q.40, a.1c; I-II, q.34, a.2, ad 1], this does not take away the fact that, as such, it is a good thing for man. It is not only good in the sense that it is useful [*bonum utile*] or something to enjoy [*bonum fruedum*]; it is also good as being something worthy [*dignum*], that is to say, something that corresponds to man's dignity, that expresses this dignity and increases it. If one wishes to define more clearly the ethical meaning of work, it is this truth that one must particularly keep in mind. Work is a good thing for man [*bonum hominis*]. . . . because through work man *not only transforms nature*. . . . but he also *achieves fulfilment* as a human being [*se ipsum ut hominem perficit*] and indeed, in a sense, becomes 'more a human being'.
>
> Without this consideration it is impossible to understand the meaning of the virtue of industriousness, and why. . . . industriousness should be a virtue: for virtue, as a moral

habit, is something whereby man becomes good as man [refers to ST., I-II, q.40, a.1c; I-II, q.34, a.2, ad 1] (LE 9).

'Toil' in this context indicates that the person's self-realisation through work in the subjective sense is *not* easy. Nevertheless, the good achieved through work is precious. The good, however, that the Pope has in mind is more important that the utility or pleasure that work may bring. The work-act *itself* is understood as a good because in and of itself it lets man *fulfil* himself by freely choosing to develop virtues, understood in the Thomist sense of the word, such as industriousness. These intransitive moral-spiritual goods are the most worthy [*dignum*] of man because they express his potential for perfection as the *imago Dei*.

In this light, one may say that much of *Laborem Exercens*' treatment of human work brings together the insights of *Gaudium et Spes* and Karol Wojtyła's own neo-Thomist thinking about human action, morality and virtue. More importantly, however, this synthesis of ideas provided Catholic social teaching with all the necessary conceptual apparatus required for a closer analysis of entrepreneurship, a step taken by John Paul II in *Sollicitudo Rei Socialis* and *Centesimus Annus*.

The Right of Private Economic Initiative

In contrast to *Laborem Exercens*, *Sollicitudo Rei Socialis* spends little time examining labour-capital relations. Instead, the Pope considers what the encyclical calls 'the right of economic initiative'. In the context of discussing the denial of human rights, *Sollicitudo Rei Socialis* states:

> It should be noted that in today's world, among other rights, *the right of economic initiative* [*inter alia iura etiam ius ad propria incepta oeconomica*] is often suppressed. Yet it is a right which is important not only for the individual but also for the common good. Experience shows us that the denial of this right, or its limitation in the name of an alleged 'equality' of everyone in society, diminishes, or in practice absolutely destroys the spirit of initiative, that is to say *the creative subjectivity of the citizen* [*subiectivam*

videlicet effectricem civis]. As a consequence, there arises not so much a true equality as a 'levelling down'. In the place of creative initiative there appears passivity, dependence and submission to the bureaucratic apparatus (SRS 15).

On one level, these words direct the Church's attention to a grave ethical flaw in state-collectivism. By suppressing personal entrepreneurship, the state denies man's very nature as a free subject; that is, the *anthropological truth* that humans are creatures capable of choosing how they act. The text above also indicates that state-collectivism necessarily stifles the *creativity* that is implicit to man's *nature* and *destiny*, as specified by the Book of Genesis. Finally, the Pope points out that the repression of personal economic initiative has negative ethical implications for society as a whole. Put simply, it necessitates the existence of a vast bureaucratic apparatus that maintains this repression while assuming for itself the role of economic development. To this extent, state-collectivism's denial of the right of economic initiative also constitutes an attack upon the common good.

There is, however, another dimension to *Sollicitudo Rei Socialis*' defence of entrepreneurship, the significance of which may not be immediately apparent. By characterising economic initiative as a right [*ius*], Pope John Paul directs attention to its significance for the possessor of rights: man. But by associating this right with man's creative subjectivity, *Sollicitudo Rei Socialis* indirectly characterises economic initiative as an *act of work* that flows from man as the *creative subject*. This has two effects. It deepens understanding of *why* entrepreneurship is a right: it expresses the truth that humans are, by nature, creative subjects of work. Secondly, it indicates that economic initiative does more than create things and benefit others. As a work-*act* of the creative subject, entrepreneurship involves man's *self-realisation* of moral good. In the cited extract above, this last point has to be inferred from John Paul's insistence that the denial of economic initiative results in the opposite of personal growth: that is, dependence and passivity. *Centesimus Annus*, however, is more forthright on this matter.

The Virtue of Entrepreneurial Activity

One of the many things for which Pope John Paul's *Centesimus Annus* will be remembered is its recognition of a decisive change in the very basis of modern capitalist economies. The Pope states, for example, that

> there are specific differences between the trends of modern society and those of the past. Whereas at one time the decisive factor of production was *the land*, and later capital. . . . today the decisive factor is increasingly *man himself*, that is, his knowledge. . . . his capacity for integrated and compact organisation, as well as his ability to perceive the needs of others and satisfy them (CA 32).

Looking, then, at the whole structure and origin of wealth, Pope John Paul indicates that land and capital are, in themselves, not enough to create wealth. The *human mind* – what Nell-Breuning called *intellectus* – is more essential than ever. Indeed, it is fundamental. As George Weigel notes, John Paul seems to regard this as a new 'sign of the times' (Weigel 1996: 139). Economic life is, from the Pope's standpoint, increasingly driven by man's capacity for insight, the habit of discerning new possibilities such as new products and services, or more efficient methods of producing or distributing goods.

John Paul II defines more precisely what he means by this increasingly 'mind-driven' state of affairs when he notes that in contemporary economic life 'the role of disciplined and creative *human work* and, as an essential part of that work, *initiative and entrepreneurial ability* [is becoming] increasingly evident and decisive [refers to SRS 15]' (CA 32). On one level, these words confirm that Pope John Paul regards economic initiative as an act of work. At the same time, by conceptualising entrepreneurship in this manner, the Pope overcomes the post-Enlightenment juxtaposition of 'capital' and 'labour' that manifested itself in Catholic social teaching as early as *Rerum Novarum*. What is 'essential' and 'decisive' is *not* the provision of 'capital' or 'labour', but rather entrepreneurial actions. Here John Paul II's words come close to constituting a Catholic affirmation of Mises' view that everyone is, in certain respects, an entrepreneur.

Moreover, by referring to the extract from *Sollicitudo Rei Socialis* cited above, Pope John Paul reminds the reader of the importance of remembering that man is the creative subject of work when thinking about entrepreneurial activities. The Pope's reason for doing so becomes more evident when he specifies that entrepreneurial activity allows people to acquire 'important virtues. . . . such as diligence, industriousness, prudence in undertaking reasonable risks, reliability and fidelity in interpersonal relationships, as well as courage in carrying out decisions which are difficult and painful' (CA 32). In an echo of *Laborem Exercens* and *The Acting Person*, John Paul indicates that the human subject's *self-realisation* of virtue through *acts* of entrepreneurial work is at least equally important as any resulting material prosperity.

In light of the preceding analysis, it does seem that Buttiglione is correct when he states that *Centesimus Annus* considers entrepreneurship to be a good in itself (Buttiglione 1992: 69). Although the material results of entrepreneurship may be grand, the greatest 'wealth' potentially created by such activity is to be found in its intransitive moral effects within human beings. Nor should it go unstated that the virtues associated by Pope John Paul with entrepreneurship mirror those underlined by St. Bernardino nearly 600 years before *Centesimus Annus*' promulgation.

This is not, however, to suggest that the Church's teaching regarding entrepreneurship is somehow 'complete'. *Centesimus Annus*, for example, only briefly addresses the third issue that the Austrian school underlines as critical to any discussion of entrepreneurial activity: that is, *why* people choose to act entrepreneurially. On this matter, the Pope has only the following to say:

> A person who produces something other than for his own use generally does so in order that others may use it after they have paid a just price, mutually agreed upon through free bargaining. It is precisely the need to foresee both the needs of others and the combination of productive factors most adapted to satisfying those needs that constitutes another important source of wealth in society (CA 32).

The word 'foresee' reminds us of Mises and Kirzner's view that entrepreneurship involves looking through the uncertainty of the future for unactualised potentialities. The Pope's words also imply that people become 'aware' of potential opportunities to create new wealth when they believe that they, as individual persons, will receive a fair price for satisfying the needs of others. Though the phrase 'self-interest' does not appear in the extract above, it seems to be the unspoken assumption underlying the Pope's analysis.

This, of course, raises other issues of even wider significance. What, for example, is the moral standing of self-interest? If, as Pope John Paul suggests, entrepreneurial activity is becoming fundamental to the production of wealth, then it may be necessary for the Catholic Church to explore this and other matters more closely.

IV. New Teaching for New Questions

As the preceding analysis illustrates, Catholic social teaching is not static. Like other aspects of Catholic doctrine, the Church's social teaching undergoes 'development'. Development in this sense, however, does not mean jettisoning past teaching and embracing whatever happens to be the latest intellectual fashion. As affirmed by the Second Vatican Council, the foundation of the Catholic Church's teaching is in the Word of God, that is, what Christians call 'Revelation', which in turn is made up of Scripture and Tradition. Taken together, the Council states, Scripture and Tradition make up 'a single sacred deposit of the Word of God, which is entrusted to the Church' (DV 10). This statement underlines the Church's commitment to the preservation and proclamation of teachings which the Church considers to be of permanent validity: what it calls the 'deposit of faith' [*depositum fidei*] in the sense of 'safe-keeping' (1 Tm 6:20; 2 Tm 1:12-14, 4:8)

Whilst emphasising the Church's responsibility to protect the *depositum fidei*, the Council states that over time

> there is a growth in insight into the realities and words that are being passed on. This comes about. . . . through the contemplation and study of believers who ponder these

things in their hearts. It comes from the intimate sense of spiritual realities which they express. And it comes from the preaching of those who have received, along with their right of succession in the episcopate, the sure charisma of truth (DV 8).

Apart from highlighting the role played by study, inner understanding, and the teaching authority of the pope and bishops in giving Revelation what Joseph Ratzinger calls its 'dynamic character' (Ratzinger 1969: 186), these words encapsulate the meaning of development. They indicate that development is not about increasing knowledge in the sense that mistakes in observation and errors in reasoning are overcome, as Revelation does not originate in human reasoning. Nor does development involve repudiating what was believed in the past. Rather, it proceeds from the fact that the linguistic formulations used by the Church do not exhaustively encapsulate the revealed truth. Hence, the Church periodically improves upon the language used in its teaching to deepen its knowledge of the truth that it possesses.

The Catholic Church often does so because it is necessary to expound its teaching in new contexts. John XXIII's opening speech to the Second Vatican Council made this very point:

This certain and unchanging teaching (i.e. Christian doctrine in its completeness), to which the faithful owe obedience, needs to be more deeply understood and set forth in ways adapted to the needs of our time. Indeed, this deposit of faith, the truths contained in our time-honoured teaching [*seu veritates, quae veneranda doctrina nostra continentur*], is one thing; the manner in which these truths are set forth (with their meaning preserved intact [*eodem tamen sensu eademque sententia*]) is something else (John XXIII 1962: 792).[8]

Development, then, involves concordance with stated teaching, but also what Rodger Charles, S.J., aptly calls 'non-contradiction' (Charles 1982: 148). This takes the form of deepening understanding

---

[8] See also GS 62. On precisely what John XXIII said, see Finnis (1991/1992).

of the teaching and setting it forth in a manner suited to the conditions of the time.

A similar process gives rise to development in the Church's social teaching. In *Sollicitudo Rei Socialis*, John Paul II states:

> following in the footsteps of my esteemed predecessors in the See of Peter [I wish] to reaffirm the *continuity* of the social doctrine as well as its constant *renewal*. . . .
>
> This twofold dimension is typical of her teaching in the social sphere. On the one hand it is *constant*, for it remains identical in its fundamental inspiration, in its 'principles of reflection', in its 'criteria of judgement', in its basic 'directives for action', and above all in its vital link with the Gospel of the Lord. On the other hand, it is ever *new*, because it is subject to the necessary and opportune adaptations suggested by the changes in historical conditions and by the unceasing flow of events which are the setting of the life of people and society (SRS 3).

The Church's acknowledgment in *Centesimus Annus* that entrepreneurship is assuming centre-place in economic life constitutes an example of such development. It results from reflection upon previous Catholic teaching concerning certain truths that the Church has proclaimed about human creativity and action, as well as a consciousness that modern economic life is increasingly driven by the mind-centred activity of entrepreneurship.

But if the Church's analysis of modern economic trends is correct, then a major change in some of the fundamental dynamics of economic life is emerging. In these new circumstances, the old conceptual framework of 'capital' and 'labour' utilised by much Catholic social teaching is no longer sufficient. Moreover, these changes raise new questions that the Church may need to address, such as the moral character of self-interest, as well as how to allow the evolution of an institutional-cultural climate that encourages as many people as possible to realise the material and moral potential of their creative subjectivity.

The Question of Self-Interest

The Austrian school insists that self-interest is crucial in alerting people to previously unknown opportunities to actualise. Without it, there is little incentive for people to take the risks often associated with entrepreneurial activity. Yet for many Christians, the very phrase 'self-interest' is anathema. The political philosopher and Christian Democrat prime minister, Amintore Fanfani, for example, was by no means a collectivist. In one of his many books, however, he did equate the pursuit of self-interest with materialism, greed, egoism and possessiveness (Fanfani 1984: 28-29).

On one level, it cannot be denied that some forms of self-interest *are* evil. As Novak suggests: 'To seek solely one's own advantage to the unfair disadvantage of others is an evil self-interest' (Novak 1992: 41). Self-interest is, in this instance, nothing more than pure egoism. One need not, however, understand self-interest only in these terms. It is not always or even commonly expressive of selfishness. Man's inclination to self-preservation is, for example, surely commendable if one regards human life, as Catholicism does, as a good in itself. Nor can a person's self-interest in their personal salvation be regarded as morally dubious. From a Christian perspective, people *should* be interested in saving their *own* souls; it is *wrong* not to be. Indeed, Aquinas held that as soon as one reaches the age of reason, one is confronted with the rational necessity of deliberating, so far as one can, about oneself [*de seipso*], and about the direction, the integrating point, of one's whole life [*salus qua*]; hence one treats oneself as an end to which other things are related as quasi-means (ST., I-II, q.89, a.6c, ad 3).

Nor can a person's interest in developing self-discipline be immediately labelled as evil. According to the Second Vatican Council, John Paul II, and numerous other Christian commentators, this form of interest in oneself is essential if one is to become truly free (GS 17; VS 42). More generally, people's actual self-interests are rarely narrowly and consistently self-obsessive. The 'self' may be 'interested' in the well-being of 'its' family and wider society. On this basis, one may conclude that although self-interest may be less than perfect, it should not be automatically condemned.

Nevertheless, there are those who suggest that Catholic social teaching has not sufficiently explored the nature of self-interest.

Daniel Finn, for instance, claims that 'John Paul II fails to analyse the moral status of self-interest, a notion central to both the critique and defence of capitalism' (Finn 1998: 667).

This statement is not, however, entirely accurate. In *Centesimus Annus*, for example, the Pope *does* consider the status of self-interest:

> man, who was created for freedom, bears within himself the wound of original sin, which constantly draws him towards evil and puts him in need of redemption. Not only is *this doctrine an integral part of Christian revelation*; it also has great hermeneutical value insofar as it helps one to understand human reality. Man tends towards good, but he is also capable of evil. He can transcend his immediate interest and still remain bound to it. The social order will be all the more stable, the more it takes this fact into account and does not place in opposition personal interest and the interests of society as a whole, but rather seeks to bring them into fruitful harmony. In fact, where self-interest is violently suppressed, it is replaced by a burdensome system of bureaucratic control which dries up the well-springs of initiative and creativity (CA 25).

Man's pursuit of self-interest, then, is not, according to the Pope, necessarily evil. Rather, it is a *reality*, a *fact* of man's nature as a creature made in God's image but weakened by original sin. Rather than indulging in the hubristic delusion that humans can build heaven on earth, the Pope adheres to what might be called the tradition of Christian realism. This is a strain of thought about social matters that manifests itself in Aquinas' claim that private property was lawful partly because 'each man is more careful to procure what is for himself alone than that which is common to many' (ST., II-II, q.66, a.2). The late-scholastic, Tomás de Mercado (1500-1575), adopted a similar position when he stated that in light of the relative scarcity [*raritas*] of goods, it was hardly surprising that 'We cannot find a person who does not favour his own interests or who does not prefer to furnish his home rather than that of the republic' (STC., II, chp.II, fol.18-19). Evidently, neither John Paul II, Aquinas, nor Mercado believe that one can ignore self-interest when thinking about how to organise economic life. Indeed, the extract from *Centesimus Annus* cited above implies that allowing people to pursue their self-interest is critical if economic initiative and creativity are to be fostered and the dead hand of collectivism avoided.

To this extent, then, one may say that Catholic teaching is already in a position to speak more frankly about the role played by self-interest in generating a person's decision to act entrepreneurially. This could, for example, involve explaining that the supreme Christian commandment of love of God and neighbour does not make acts of economic initiative driven by self-interest *ipso facto* morally questionable. It would also be useful for the Church to delineate some of the distinctions between self-interest and selfishness, highlighting where the former degenerates into the latter.

An Entrepreneurial Culture

If, as *Centesimus Annus* suggests, entrepreneurial activity is a morally virtuous habit, then one is bound to consider how this habit is nurtured by a society's culture and institutions. The failed experiment of socialism illustrates that a society's political-economic culture can have lasting effects upon individuals' behaviour-patterns. This was certainly the view of one of Poland's leading Catholic intellectuals, Józef Tischner, as he reflected upon the state of post-Communist societies in 1991:

> Totalitarian rule consists in subordination and creates subordinates. After its fall, old habits do not disappear. You can see inscriptions on city walls in Poland saying 'Commies – come back!!' Their authors are people of whom the liberalisation of the economy and politics demand something they are incapable of – a personal responsibility for their own actions. Communism's material ravages are small compared with the devastation of the internal, spiritual world of the individual (Tischner 1991: 165-166).

Put another way, the decidedly 'unfree' system of Communism presupposed and effected a suppression of personal responsibility.

Unfortunately, the dissolution of state-collectivism will not, in itself, automatically change such behaviour. Addressing the Czech parliament seven years later in 1998, Václav Havel, the outstanding advocate of freedom and truth in Communist Czechoslovakia and its first post-Communist President, expressed a similar opinion: 'along with Communism, the structure of daily values held in place by the system for decades collapsed overnight. . . . The time of certainties, as false as these certainties were, gave way to freedom. With it, completely new demands were placed on individual responsibility, and many found this responsibility unbearable' (Havel 1998: 42).

On the basis of these experiences, it may be suggested that while developments in economic life in the late twentieth century have made economic life more mind-centred, the proliferation of entrepreneurship remains, to a large extent, dependent upon cultural, economic, and political systems that affirm free economic initiative. Has Catholic social teaching fully grasped this point? Certainly, John Paul II has repeatedly stressed that economic creativity is stifled by state-collectivism. But it is arguable that entrepreneurship can be significantly subdued in more subtle ways, even in relatively free economies.

This, of course, is not to suggest that every aspect of social life should be subordinated to the promotion of entrepreneurship. There are some forms of entrepreneurial activity, such as selling gas chambers for use in extermination camps or marketing oneself as an assassin, that no Christian can ever accept as legitimate forms of enterprise. Like any other freely willed human act, entrepreneurial activity must not, from a Catholic perspective, directly contradict Scripture and/or the natural law or contribute to the gross violation of their precepts. Catholic ethics has, nevertheless, also perennially recognised that human (positive) law cannot and ought not try to forbid every single evil action (Copleston 1976: 240). Aquinas, for example, wrote that human law rightly refrains from suppressing some vices. In his view, it should only forbid those vices which would render human society impossible: 'thus human law prohibits murder, theft, and such like' (ST., I-II, q.96, a2). His reason for stating this is simple: much that is useful would be prevented if all sins were strictly prohibited [*multae utiltates impedirentur si omnia peccata districte prohiberentur*] (ST., II-II, q.78, a.1, ad.3).

Given, however, the Church's renewed attention to private economic initiative, it is reasonable to hope that it will ask more questions about how societies might enhance the amount of entrepreneurial activity. Once again, the Austrians may be in a position to offer much guidance to Catholic thinkers in relation to this subject. In the first instance, Kirzner points out that if entrepreneurial discovery-orientated processes are accepted as the key to economic growth, it becomes difficult to see wealth-creation 'as a phenomenon best achieved through deliberate planning [because it] inevitably clamps economic growth into a framework from which open-ended discovery is excluded'. Indeed, Kirzner suggests that 'to plan presumes that the framework within which planning takes place is already fully discovered' (Kirzner 1985: 71). Although one may wonder whether this presumption is always true (not all plans presuppose that frameworks are stable), there seems little question that planning, be it of a 'neo-Keynesian' or profoundly statist character, cannot account for the unpredictability and dynamism generated by millions of on-going individual entrepreneurial acts. Faced with this reality, governments are perennially tempted to try and limit this dynamism and creativity, precisely because it makes economic planning seem more viable.

Catholic social teaching has always maintained that government does have a role to play in economic life. Since 1891, however, there have been some distinct differences in emphasis in teaching about the state's economic role. In *Rerum Novarum*, for example, Leo XIII articulated a rather minimalist view (RN 4, 7, 12-15, 32-40). By contrast, Paul VI stated in *Populorum Progressio* that 'It pertains to the public authorities to choose, even to lay down the objectives to be pursued, the ends to be achieved, and the means for achieving these, and it is for them to stimulate all the forces engaged in this common activity' (PP 33). Though Pope Paul qualified this remark by warning that private enterprise should always be associated with state-planning so as to 'avoid the danger of complete collectivisation'

(PP 33), this view of the state's economic role leaves little room for the spontaneous creativity and unpredictability generated by entrepreneurial activity.

In more recent decades, Catholic social teaching has placed less emphasis upon the type of planning advocated by Paul VI and shifted towards describing the state's primary economic responsibility as the provision and maintenance of an institutional and juridical framework within which free economic activity can occur (CA 48). Even when it comes to protecting human rights in the economic sector, John Paul II has stressed that 'primary responsibility in this area belongs not to the State but to individuals and to the various groups and associations that make up society' (CA 48). Though insisting that the state has a responsibility to prevent the development of monopolies and may 'in exceptional circumstances. . . . exercise a *substitute function*, when social sectors or business systems are too weak or just getting under way', *Centesimus Annus* maintains that such interventions must be 'as brief as possible, so as to avoid removing permanently from society and business systems the functions that are properly theirs, and enlarging excessively the sphere of State intervention to the detriment of both economic and civil freedom' (CA 48).

Each of these statements reflect a consciousness, at least on the Papacy's part, that one of the painful lessons of the twentieth century is that even moderate state economic-planning can have unforeseen negative consequences for free societies. John Paul II's underlining of some of the welfare state's dysfunctional outcomes is another example of this awareness (CA 48).

It may, however, be the case that Catholic social teaching needs to consider how other aspects of state intervention may indirectly discourage people from acting entrepreneurially. Austrians such as Kirzner believe that regulatory measures such as tariffs, licensing requirements, labour legislation, etc., 'do not merely limit numbers in particular markets. These kinds of regulatory activity tend to bar entrepreneurs who believe that they have discovered profit opportunities in barred areas of the market' (Kirzner 1983: 78). Moreover, as Hayek demonstrates, there is much evidence to suggest that such regulatory measures significantly distort the workings of the competitive price system which act as a discovery procedure for entrepreneurs. Consequently, many potential opportunities for wealth-creation simply remain undiscovered (Hayek 1978).

Nor will entrepreneurial activity be sufficiently forthcoming if there is not sufficient incentive to elicit the necessary insights and encourage people to take risks. Taxation rates, of course, can have potentially negative or positive effects upon this incentive. As Kirzner notes: 'To announce in advance to potential entrepreneurs that "lucky" profits will be taxed away is to convert open-ended situations into situations more and more approximating those of a given, closed character' (Kirzner 1985: 111). In such circumstances, the incentive for entrepreneurs to pay attention to anything save *that which is already known* is removed; this development consequently dries up the well-springs of alertness to potential entrepreneurial opportunities to create new wealth.

If one examines the documents of Catholic social teaching, it soon becomes apparent that they contain little detailed examination of such matters. Given, however, the Papal magisterium's insistence that entrepreneurship is central to wealth-creation, it is difficult to see how Catholic social teaching can avoid giving closer consideration to what practices discourage entrepreneurial acts, inhibit economic creativity, limit markets to established monopolies, and circumscribe the poor's ability to realise the potential of their creative subjectivity.

Moving from the institutional to the more directly cultural, the creation of an entrepreneurial-friendly climate also involves shaping the attitudes of people towards business and entrepreneurs. It is right and good that we celebrate the achievements of scientists, artists, and scholars. But do civil society and the state give the same recognition to those who are the primary initiators of the processes that provide us with the material basis of our existence? While the Catholic Church has never hesitated to praise trade unions' accomplishments (QA 31-36; LE 20; CA 15, 26), Catholic social teaching has rarely lauded businesspeople for the moral and material fruits of their deeds.

Throughout his pontificate, John Paul II has made efforts to correct this imbalance. During a 1983 address in Milan, for example, the Pope pointed out: 'The degree of well-being which society enjoys today would be unthinkable without the dynamic figure of the businessman, whose function consists of organising labour and the means of production so as to give rise to the goods and services necessary for the prosperity and progress of the community' (John Paul II 1983: 9). Similarly, in a speech to businessmen in Spain, the Pope stated:

> Do not fall into the temptation to give up business, to shut down, to devote yourselves egotistically to calmer and less demanding professional activities. Overcome such temptations to escape, and keep bravely at your posts. . . . keeping in mind the great contribution you make to the common good when you open up fresh work opportunities.
>
> Major errors were committed by entrepreneurs during the development of the Industrial Revolution in the past. But that is no reason for failing, dear industrialists, to give public recognition and praise to your dynamism, your spirit of initiative, your iron wills, your creative capacities and your ability to take risks. These qualities have made you key figures in economic history, and in confronting the future (John Paul II 1982: 375).

Such direct praise of entrepreneurs is, however, virtually non-existent at the encyclical level of Catholic social teaching. Even *Centesimus Annus* limits itself to applauding entrepreneurial activity rather than the *person* of the entrepreneur himself.

Yet it is precisely this type of affirmation from autonomous cultural institutions such as the Catholic Church that is necessary if people are going to be encouraged to learn the moral habits that are at the heart of entrepreneurial wealth-creation. For why should people want to learn the combination of virtues of prudent risk-taking, industriousness, courage, firmness, and diligence that the Church regards as pertinent to the emergence and sustaining of entrepreneurial activity, if they are also subtly encouraged to view entrepreneurs in generally negative terms or as simply performing an important but morally-neutral function? As a 2000 year-old institution whose mission is to teach the Truth about God and man rather than win immediate popularity contests, the Catholic Church may need to move from praising entrepreneurial activity *per se* to a more explicit affirmation of people who embrace this activity as their *vocation*.

V. Conclusion: A Noble Vocation

It is not an exaggeration to say that the recovery of entrepreneurship within the Catholic tradition has placed the Church in a better position to reflect upon the new economic world emerging at the beginning of the third Christian millennium. But of possibly greater importance is the manner in which this rediscovery has allowed the Catholic Church to remind us that the greatest economic resource of all is not capital or land, but rather the human person.

This is one of the truths highlighted by *Centesimus Annus*: 'Not only has God given the earth to man, who must use it with respect for the original good purpose for which it was given to him, but man too is God's gift to man' (CA 38). People are not just consumers: they are also beings that think, act, and create – this is a profoundly Judeo-Christian insight traceable to the very first page of the very first chapter of the very first book of the Hebrew and Christian Scriptures. Thus, one may say that while, from a Catholic perspective, the call to be an entrepreneur may not be quite as sublime as, for example, the call of parenthood, it is nevertheless a noble vocation. As Robert Sirico writes: 'It requires those who pursue it to be watchful practitioners in the art of discovery, for by it they will create employment opportunities for those who would otherwise go without' (Sirico 1991: 6). By themselves, brilliant ideas do not serve mankind. If they are to serve humanity, they must be transformed by complex processes of design, organisation, and production. The capacity to combine all of these talents and actions is rare. But if entrepreneurs are faithful to this call, then the Lord will say to them at the end of time, just as He said to the creative servants in Matthew's Gospel: 'Well done, good and faithful servant; you have shown that you can be faithful in small things, I will trust you with greater; come and share in your Master's happiness'.

Abbreviations

C A	*Centesimus Annus*
Con	*Confessions*, Book (I) and Chapter (1)
DII	*De Iustitia de Iure*, Book (VI), Question (q.2), and Article (a.2).
D V	*Dei Verbum*
ES	*Ecclesiam Suam*
G S	*Gaudium et Spes*
L C	*Libertatis Conscientia*
L E	*Laborem Exercens*
N E	*Nicomachean Ethics*, Book (II) and Section (1).
Pol	*Politics*, Book (I) and Section (1)
P P	*Populorum Progressio*
Q A	*Quadragesimo Anno*
R N	*Rerum Novarum*
ScG	*Summa contra Gentiles*, Book (I), Chapter (chp.6), and paragraph number (n.1)
SRS	*Sollicitudo Rei Socialis*
S T	*Summa Theologiae*, Part (I–II), Question (q.64), and Article (a.1); (a.1c = body of the reply in a.1; ad 4. = reply to fourth objection in relevant article).
STC	*Summa de Tratos y Contratos*, Book (II), Chapter (chp.II), and folio (fol.18).
VS	*Veritatis Splendor*[9]

---

[9] Number following CA, DV, ES, GS, LC, LE, PP, QA, RN, SRS and VS refers to paragraph number.

Bibliography

Aquinas, St. Thomas. 1975, *Summa Theologiae*, Blackfriars, London.

Aristotle. 1976a, *The Nicomachean Ethics*, tr. J. Thomson, Penguin, London.

——. 1976b, *Politics*, tr. J. Thomson, Penguin, London.

Augustine, St. 1961, *Confessions*, tr. R.S. Pine-Coffin, Penguin, London.

Armstrong, J. 1993, 'One Protestant looks at *Centesimus Annus*', *Journal of Business Ethics* 12 (12): 933-944.

Bauer, P. 1982, 'An Economist Replies: Ecclesiastical Economics is Envy Exalted', *This World* 1: 65-74.

Bernardino of Siena, St. 1591/1928, *Opera Omnia*, Fordham University Press, New York.

Bigongiari, D., ed. 1981, *The Political Ideas of St. Thomas Aquinas*, Hafner Press, New York.

Brown, L.C. 1967, 'Natural Law in Economics', *New Catholic Encyclopedia*, McGraw-Hill, New York.

Buttiglione, R. 1992, 'The Free Economy and the Free Man', in *A New Worldly Order: John Paul II and Human Freedom – A 'Centesimus Annus' Reader*, ed. G. Weigel, Ethics and Public Policy Center, Washington, D.C.

——. 1997, *Karol Wojtyła: The Thought of the Man Who Became John Paul II*, Eerdmans, Cambridge.

Charles S.J., R. 1982, *The Social Teaching of Vatican II: Its Origins and Development. Catholic Social Ethics – A Historical and Comparative Study*, Plater Press/Ignatius Press, Oxford/San Francisco.

——. 1998, *Christian Social Witness and Teaching: The Catholic Tradition – From 'Genesis' to 'Centesimus Annus'*, 2 vols., Gracewing, Leominister.

Chenu O.P., M-D. 1986, 'A Council for all Peoples', in *Vatican II: By Those Who Were There*, ed. A. Stacpoole, O.S.B., G. Chapman, London.

Clark, J.B. 1899, *The Distribution of Wealth*, Macmillan, London.

Congregation for the Doctrine of the Faith. 1986, *Libertatis Conscientia*, Catholic Truth Society, London.

Copleston S.J., F. 1976, *Thomas Aquinas*, Search Press, London.

Daniel-Rops, H. 1964, *The Church in the Eighteenth Century*, Darton, Longman and Todd, London.

Fanfani, A. 1933, *Le Origini dello Spirituo Capitalistico in Italia*, Vita et Pensiero, Milan.

——. 1984, *Catholicism, Protestantism and Capitalism*, University of Notre Dame Press, Notre Dame.

Ferguson, A. 1767/1966, *An Essay on the History of Civil Society*, ed. D. Forbes, T. Clark and Sons, Edinburgh.

Finn, D. 1998, 'John Paul II and the Moral Ecology of Markets', *Theological Studies* 59: 662-679.

Finnis, J. 1991/1992, 'Letters to the Editor', *The Tablet*, 14 December 1991: 1544-1545; 4 January 1992: 14; 18 January 1992: 70-71; 1 February 1992: 140; 8 February 1992: 170.

——. 1998, *Aquinas: Moral, Political, and Legal Theory*, Oxford University Press, Oxford.

Fisher, M. 1983, 'The Entrepreneur, the Economist and Public Policy', in *The Entrepreneur in Society*, Centre for Independent Studies, Sydney.

Gini, A. 1992, 'Meaningful Work and the Rights of the Workers', *Thought* 67 (266): 225-239.

Grice-Hutchinson, M. 1952, *The School of Salamanca: Readings in Spanish Monetary Theory*, Clarendon Press, Oxford.

Griffiths, B. 1984, *The Creation of Wealth*, Hodder and Stoughton, London.

Gronbacher, G. 1998, 'The Need for Economic Personalism', *Journal of Markets and Morality* 1 (1): 1-34.

Havel, V. 1998, 'The State of the Republic', *New York Review of Books* 45 (4): 42-46

Hayek, F.A. von. 1944/1992, 'Historians and the Future of Europe', *The Fortunes of Liberalism: Essays on Austrian Economics and the Ideal of Freedom*, ed. P. Klein, University of Chicago Press, Chicago.

——. 1947/1992, 'Opening Address to a Conference at Mont Pèlerin'. In *The Fortunes of Liberalism*.

——. 1953, 'The Actonian Revival', *The Freeman*, March 2: 461-462.

——. 1960, *The Constitution of Liberty*, Routledge and Kegan Paul,

London.
——. 1978, *New Studies in Philosophy, Politics, Economics and the History of Ideas*, Routledge and Kegan Paul, London.
——. 1988, *The Fatal Conceit: The Errors of Socialism*, ed. W. Bartley, University of Chicago Press, Chicago.
——. 1994, *Hayek on Hayek: An Autobiographical Dialogue*, ed. S. Kresge and L. Wenar, University of Chicago Press, Chicago.
Hicks, J.R. and Weber, W., eds. 1973, *Carl Menger and the Austrian School of Economics*, Clarendon Press, Oxford.
Hsia, R. Po-Chia. 1998, *The World of Catholic Renewal 1540-1770*, Cambridge University Press, Cambridge.
John XXIII. 1962, 'Address at the Opening of Vatican II', *Acta Apostolicae Sedis* 54: 786-795.
John Paul II. 1981, *Laborem Exercens*, Catholic Truth Society, London.
——. 1982, 'The Gospel of Work', *Origins*, 18 November: 375-376
——. 1983, 'Man and his Values are the Principle and Aim of Economics', *L'Osservatore Romano*, 20 June: 9-10.
——. 1987, *Sollicitudo Rei Socialis*, Catholic Truth Society, London.
——. 1991, *Centesimus Annus*, Catholic Truth Society, London.
——. 1993, *Veritatis Splendor*, Catholic Truth Society, London.
Johnson, P. 1976, *A History of Christianity*, Penguin, London.
Kaufmann, F-X. 1997, 'Religion and Modernization in Europe', *Journal of Institutional and Theoretical Economics* 153 (1): 80-96.
Kirzner, I. 1983, 'The Primacy of Entrepreneurial Discovery', in *The Entrepreneur in Society*, Centre for Independent Studies, Sydney.
——. 1985, *Discovery and the Capitalist Process*, University of Chicago Press, Chicago.
——. 1989, *Discovery, Capitalism, and Distributive Justice*, Basil Blackwell, Oxford.
Knight, F. 1921, *Uncertainty and Profit*, Houghton Mifflin, Boston.
Leibenstein, H. 1978, *General X-Efficiency Theory and Economic Development*, Oxford University Press, Oxford.
Leo XIII. 1891, *Rerum Novarum*, in C. Carlen, I.H.M., ed. 1981, *The Papal Encyclicals*, Vol. 2, McGrath Publishing, Ann Arbor.
MacIntyre, A. 1981, *After Virtue: A Study in Moral Theory*, University of Notre Dame Press, Notre Dame.

Menger, C. 1871/1923, *Grundsätze der Volkwirtschaftlehre*, Vol. 1 (2nd ed.), Hölder-Pichler-Tempsky, Vienna.

Mercado, T. de. 1571/1975, *Summa de Tratos y Contratos*, Editoria Nacional, Madrid.

Mises, L. von. 1933/1981, *Epistemological Problems of Economics*, tr. G. Reisman, New York University Press, New York and London.

——. 1966, *Human Action: A Treatise on Economics* (3rd rev.ed.), Henry Regnery, Chicago.

——. 1981, *Socialism*, Liberty Press, Indianapolis.

——. 1985, *Liberalism in the Classical Tradition*, tr. R. Raico, Foundation for Economic Education, New York.

Misner, P. 1991, *Social Catholicism in Europe: From the Onset of Industrialisation to the First World War*, Darton, Longman and Todd, London.

Nell-Breuning S.J., O. von. 1969, 'Socio-Economic Life', in *Commentary on the Documents of Vatican II*, ed. H. Vorgrimler, Vol. V, Herder and Herder, New York.

Noonan, J. 1957, *The Scholastic Analysis of Usury*, Harvard University Press, Cambridge.

Novak, M. 1989, *Free Persons and the Common Good*, Madison Books, New York.

——. 1992, *This Hemisphere of Liberty: A Philosophy of the Americas*, AEI Press, Washington, D.C.

Paul VI. 1964, *Ecclesiam Suam*, in C. Carlen, I.H.M., ed. 1981, *The Papal Encyclicals*, Vol. 5, McGrath Publishing, Ann Arbor.

——. 1967, *Populorum Progressio*, in C. Carlen, I.H.M., ed. 1981, *The Papal Encyclicals*, Vol. 5, McGrath Publishing, Ann Arbor.

Pell, G. 1992, '*Rerum Novarum*: One Hundred Years Later', A modified version of a paper originally presented at the first *Boston Conversazione*, Spring 1991, held at The Castle, Boston University, 4 February 1991.

Pera O.P., C. ed. 1961, *S. Thomae Aquinatis De Veritate Catholicae Fidei contra Errores Infidelium (Summa contra Gentiles)*, Marietti, Turin.

Ratzinger, J. 1969, 'The Transmission of Divine Revelation', in

Commentary on the Documents of Vatican II, ed. H. Vorgrimler, Vol. IV, Herder and Herder, London.

Robertson, H. 1973, *Aspects of the Rise of Economic Individualism: A Criticism of Max Weber and His School*, A.M. Kelly, Clifton.

Roover, R. de. 1963, 'The Scholastic Attitude toward Trade and Entrepreneurship', *Explorations in Entrepreneurial History* 2: 76-87.

——. 1967, 'The Scholastics, Usury, and Foreign Exchange', *Business History Review* 41: 257-271.

Saravía de la Calle, L. 1544/1949, *Instrucción de Mercaderes muy Provechosa*, IEP, Madrid.

Schultz, T. 1975, 'The Value of the Ability to Deal with Disequilibrium', *Journal of Economic Literature* 13 (3): 827-846.

Schumpeter, J. 1950, *Capitalism, Socialism and Democracy* (3rd ed.), Harper and Row, New York.

Second Vatican Council. 1965a, Dogmatic Constitution on Divine Revelation *Dei Verbum*, in A. Flannery, O.P., gen. ed. 1988, *Vatican Council II: The Conciliar and Post Conciliar Documents*, Vol. 1 (rev. ed.), Fowler Wright Books Ltd., Leominister.

——. 1965b, Pastoral Constitution on the Church in the Modern World *Gaudium et Spes*, in *Vatican Council II*.

Sirico, R. 1991, 'The Entrepreneurial Vocation', *Religion and Liberty* 1 (5): 1, 4-6.

Soto O.P., D. de. 1540/1968, *De Iustitia de Iure*, IEP, Madrid.

Tischner, J. 1991, 'A View from the Ruins', in *A New Worldly Order: John Paul II and Human Freedom – A 'Centesimus Annus' Reader*, ed. G. Weigel, Ethics and Public Policy Center, Washington, D.C.

Vaughn, K. 1994, *Austrian Economics in America: The Migration of a Tradition*, Cambridge University Press, Cambridge.

Weigel, G. 1996, *Soul of the World: Notes on the Future of Public Catholicism*, Ethics and Public Policy Center, Washington, D.C.

Wieser, F. von. 1927, *Social Economics*, Allen and Unwin, London.

Wojtyła, K. 1977, 'Il problema del costituirsi della cultura attraverso la praxis umana', *Rivista de Filosofia Neo-Scolastica* 69 (3): 513-524.

——. 1979a, *The Acting Person*, tr. A. Potocki, Reidel Publishing, Dordrecht. Originally published as Wojtyła, K. 1969, *Osoba i Czyn*, Polskie Towarzystwo Teologiczne, Kraków.

——. 1979b, 'The Person: Subject and Community', *Review of Metaphysics* 33: 273-301. Originally published as Wojtyła, K. 1976, 'Osoba: podmiot i wspólnota', *Roczniki Filozoficzne* 24 (2): 5-39.

Woźnicki, A. 1986, 'Lublinism: A New Version of Thomism', *Proceedings of the American Catholic Philosophical Association* 58: 27-37.

Index

Religion and the Free Society:

Educating the Churches in the Principles and Processes of the Free Economy

The CIS's *Religion and the Free Society* programme seeks to provide clergy, theologians, and lay church workers with a better understanding of economics, as well as an appreciation of the principles and workings of the free economy and virtuous society. In the longer term, the programme hopes to help alter the current consensus of thinking within the churches about economics, so that, at a minimum, there will be a growth in religious thinking about wealth creation and distribution. The programme seeks to achieve this end by:

• *Theological-Economic Research*. This includes building a positive corpus of religious thinking about the free economy and society, the holding of the CIS's annual Acton Lecture on Religion and Freedom, as well as occasional lectures, workshops, and seminars.

• *Educating Future Religious Leaders and Thinkers*. This occurs through the holding of Free Society conferences for those training for future ministry, theologians, church workers, etc., during which they are given an introduction to economics as well as the theological-philosophical premises of the free and virtuous society.

• *Educating Present Religious Leaders and Thinkers*. As well as organising seminars for economists, businesspersons, and religious leaders, the CIS produces responses to church economic statements. These responses underline any flaws in the empirical evidence or basic economic reasoning used by such documents, and, where appropriate, critique their theological and philosophical premises. Alternative arguments that provide theological support for the thinking and practices underlying the free economy and virtuous society are also expressed.

**To learn more, visit our website at http://www.cis.org.au
or contact the CIS on (02) 9438 4377, Fax (02) 9439 7310**

Recent CIS Publications from Religion and the Free Society

Catholicism and the Architecture of Freedom
George Pell
Delivered as the Inaugural Acton Lecture on Religion and Freedom, this Occasional Paper by George Pell examines the meaning of freedom in modern society, and the contributions that religion can make to ensuring that freedom does not become detached from truth.
[OP70]   ISBN   1 8 6 4 3 2 0 4 4 3   (1999)   24pp

Religion and Liberty.
Western Experiences, Asian Possibilities
Samuel Gregg
The Occasional Paper was first delivered at the Mont Pèlerin Society Meeting in Indonesia, 1999. It examines religion's impact upon the development of liberty in the West, and speculates upon religion's potential efects upon the growth of freedom in Asia.
[OP68]   ISBN   1 8 6 4 3 2 0 4 2 7   (1999)   44pp

In Praise of the Free Economy
Essays by Michael Novak
Edited by Samuel Gregg
This collection of essays by the American theologian-philosopher Michael Novak illustrates that it is entirely possible to be a Christian and in favour of free enterprise, markets and a limited state.
[R10]   ISBN   1 8 6 4 3 2 0 4 0 0   (1999)   118pp

To order these books, visit our website at
www.cis.org.au
or contact the CIS on
Ph (02) 9438 4377, Fax (02) 9439 7310

STATE OF THE NATION 1999
Indicators of a Changing Australia

Lucy Sullivan • Jennifer Buckingham • Barry Maley • Helen Hughes

This new edition of State of the Nation expands and updates the original edition (from 1997) with a comprehensive look at Australia. Developments over the past century are looked at in terms of various social, economic, cultural and recreational measures.

An authoritative reference for the scholar, student, or casual reader interested in an easily read and understood snapshot of Australia today

[SP02]   ISBN   1 8 6 4 3 2 0 4 1 9   (1999)   160pp

ORDER IT NOW!
A$24.95
(not including postage & handling)

Recent CIS Publications

ildren's Rights
ere the Law is Heading and What it Means for Families
ry Maley

ry Maley examines the evolution of family law over the past few years
argues that the imposition of a changing set of legal infrastructure has
ved counterproductive for the traditional family. He also maintains
the autonomy of the family unit is under threat from developments
1 as the United Nations Conventions on the Rights of the Child.
\43]   ISBN   1 8 6 4 3 2 0 3 8 9   (1999)   132pp

Reconnecting Compassion and Charity
Roger Kerr

This Occasional Paper looks at the relationship between charity and
compassion, and suggests that the present reliance on the state to do chari-
table work should make way for a return to genuine compassion at an
individual level and greater personal involvement in charity.
[OP67]   ISBN   1 8 6 4 3 2 0 3 9 7   (1999)   20pp

Modern Mask of Socialism:
onio Martino

ginally presented as the Fifteenth Annual John Bonython Lecture,
onio Martino argues that socialism in the old sense is indeed dead, but
socialism has taken on new forms that need to be challenged.
'66]   ISBN   1 8 6 4 3 2 0 3 7 0   (1998)   32pp

To order these books, visit our website at
www.cis.org.au
or contact the CIS on
Ph (02) 9438 4377, Fax (02) 9439 7310